Merry Christmas, America!

Merry Christmas, America!

Megawatt Displays Across the U.S.A.

BRUCE LITTLEFIELD

COLLINS | DESIGN

An Imprint of HarperCollinsPublishers

HarperCollins books may be purchased for educational, business, or sales promotional use.
For information, please write: Special Markets Department, HarperCollins Publishers,
10 East 53rd Street, New York, NY 10022.

First Edition

First published in 2007 by:
Collins Design,
An Imprint of HarperCollins*Publishers*
10 East 53rd Street
New York, NY 10022
Tel: (212) 207-7000
Fax: (212) 207-7654
collinsdesign@harpercollins.com
www.harpercollins.com

Distributed throughout the world by:
HarperCollins*Publishers*
10 East 53rd Street
New York, NY 10022
Fax: (212) 207-7654

Design by Kay Schuckhart/Blond on Pond

Library of Congress Cataloging-in-Publication Data

Littlefield, Bruce (Bruce Duanne)
  Merry Christmas, America! : megawatt displays across the U.S.A. /
Bruce Littlefield. -- 1st ed.
     p. cm.
  ISBN-13: 978-0-06-134829-7 (pbk.)
  ISBN-10: 0-06-134829-5 (pbk.)
  1. Christmas--United States. 2. United States--Social life and
customs. I. Title.

GT4986.A1L58 2007
394.26630973--dc22

2007018743

Printed in China
First Printing, 2007

To my mother, who got over the plastic Santa

Contents

Introduction

Christmas makes us happy like no other holiday. It's downright fun, except at one-day sales and during light detangling, and presents a chance to become a child again, color outside the lines, and throw a little twinkle around, whether it's our typical nature or not. A lot of us go all out, using our houses as a painter would a canvas, turning normally shy facades into colorful, brightly lit statements, some so dazzling airline pilots note them as landmarks from thirty thousand feet.

These are the houses in our neighborhoods we all know—glittering, three-dimensional Christmas cards

that shout Joy to the world! These are the homes where the enthusiastic elves live—you know, the people who peel October off the calendar as if it's a challenger's gauntlet and have their lists checked twice before the rest of us have gotten through Halloween. These holly haulers spend weeks, sometimes months, planning, prepping, and purchasing, and days untangling, unfurling, and unpacking so that they can give the rest of us an illuminated, inflated, animated gift.

America began tripping the electric light fantastic rather simply on December 22, 1882, in the apartment of Edward H. Johnson, an inventor and the business partner of Thomas Edison. In a spirited burst of ingenuity, Johnson designed eighty red, white, and blue electric light bulbs the size of walnuts and displayed them on the Christmas tree in his Fifth Avenue apartment in New York City. Christmas was dark nevermore.

Christmas is a time when everybody wants his past forgotten and his present remembered. What I don't like about office Christmas parties is looking for a job the next day.

—Phyllis Diller

In 1895, when Grover Cleveland was president, the White House displayed the first electrically lit Christmas tree. The tree featured more than a hundred multicolored lights and was a huge hit, leading the Edison General Electric Company to introduce America to the first strand of Christmas tree lights. The following year, Christmas light parties were the rage among fashionable high society, as the well-to-do showed off their three-hundred-dollar lighted trees. Then, in December 1901, the advertisement for General Electric's stringed lights with nine sockets appeared in the *Ladies' Home Journal,* and a buying frenzy ensued. Even though the lights were expensive (twelve dollars a strand), it didn't matter. An electrically lit tree became the instant must-have status symbol.

By the late 1920s, General Electric had begun sponsoring neighborhood "decorating-with-color-light" contests to spark interest in and encourage sales of its new outdoor Christmas lights. Newspapers covered the competition, featuring colorful houses and their proud owners, and the enthusiasm for full-frontal decorating took off. After World War II, the passionate interest in Christmas illumination and decoration grew enthusiastically, almost fanatically, and today the paraphernalia is practically as limitless as the imagination.

It's hard to resist plugging into Christmas. Each year, two out of every three families buy new baubles to deck their halls, collectively spending an estimated nine billion dollars in the process. Then families take to the floors of their living rooms, adding the newly acquired bags of Christmas present to the boxes filled with those of Christmas past, and they begin figuring out the schematics. They carefully unpack their heirlooms, each a memory of another time, then take on the monumental task of detangling the wiry webs that are the keystone of holiday displays.

Yes, the lights. Stashed haphazardly into bags sometime after the New Year, they are plugged in each holiday season; and inevitably, one in their lineage is imperceptibly unhitched from its socket. Like socks that disappear in the dryer, they are a mystery that may never be solved. Despite years of industrial engineering and millions of dollars in research and development, there's often a confounding strand that has lost its twinkle, refuses to spark, and leaves us running to the store for more.

My first memory of Christmas is of electric lights—electric being the key word. I was three years old, tinkering with lights beneath the bottom branches of a scrawny fir in my grandmother's living room.

In rural South Carolina, trees were plucked from wherever they could be found, and my grandmother typically found hers somewhere along the railroad tracks behind her house. Every year, around Thanksgiving, she'd head down past her pecan trees, saw in one hand, my hand in the other, to find a scrawny specimen. In later years, after she'd snatched every sapling—from the depot a quarter mile to the north to the bridge a quarter mile to the south—she resorted to roadside nabbing, which she'd perform during one of her infamous saw-in-the-trunk shortcuts. My grandfather always drove the getaway car.

Each year after the hack job, she'd drag the thirsty thing back up to the house, stick it in a wrought iron stand, and pour it a cocktail of ginger ale and water (we were teetotalers, so the tree should be too). First came the lights. They were big and colorful. And, as I'd discover later, searingly hot.

But my first Christmas memory is sticking the prongs of the plug into the outlet, along with my forefinger. The memory is still shocking: stunningly, staggeringly electric. Think Phyllis Diller hair, and tears that burst forth like rain from an angry cloud.

Several years later, I had forgiven the lights, and my mother had become fast friends with a "crafty" sort named Judy McChesney. It was not uncommon to see McCall's pantsuit patterns spread out on the shag rug of the McChesneys' living room and elaborate cross-stitch scenes framed on their walls. I remember arriving at Judy's ornament-decorating festivities and being instantly struck by the divergence of red, gold, and green splashed against 1970s orange and avocado.

Hers was a Christmas in swank Technicolor. But nothing could have been as exciting to my six-year-old eyes than a stack of ribbon and a box filled with enough sequins and sparkly things to cover a Bob Mackie gown.

We made ornaments for hours, singing "Jingle Bells" at least a thousand times. It was the first song I could sing and still runs neck-in-neck with the pa-rum-pum-pum-pumming "Little Drummer Boy" as a personal favorite. To this day, the bejeweled Styrofoam ornaments my mother and I made at the McChesneys' remain as favorites in our vast and ever-expanding collections.

As I grew older, my vision of the Christmas experience expanded—to outside our house—where it could be seen beneath the glare of the yard lights and the watchful eyes of judgmental neighbors. Bigger definitely became better. One year, the first year of the neighborhood Christmas decorating contest, I wrapped our house like a present. With a tall ladder, and bolts and bolts of "imperfect" red nylon from the textile plant where my dad worked, I made our house the biggest "present" in the neighborhood. I tied a giant bow across our front door rendering it completely unusable during the holiday season. Though I didn't win the decorating contest, I did get my picture in the paper as the kid who "tried to wrap his house."

A couple of years later, in another failed attempt to win the "Best House" award and its congratulatory red-lettered sign, I made a tableau in which it appeared that Santa had fallen off our house into the giant molding leaf pile in our front yard. How the Nickels, with their understated Charlestonian pineapple-candle-in-each-window routine, beat my Santa-legs-and-black-boots-sticking-out-of-a-leaf-pile-and-flailing-about-in-the-breeze concept, is beyond me. But it did. Perhaps if we had snow in South Carolina mine would have been a little more compelling.

I never won the "Best House" award. But that didn't—or hasn't—stopped my Christmas decorating. I'm happy to live in the shadow of others who feel that anything worth doing is worth doing over the top. These are the true believers. These are the people who electrify the holiday and go all out to make every Christmas the brightest, merriest, happiest Christmas ever.

Visitors flock to these glimmering exhibits like fine art aficionados to the unveiling of a rare Rembrandt, driving slowly by in packed vehicles to gawk at the wonder of colorful characters and puffy blow-up figures. Children beg to get closer, and adults, lost in the magic of the moment, humor them, parking their cars haphazardly along highways and byways to rush over and get a close-up view of Christmas.

It's pure delight. Every last blinking moment of it.

But who are these people who take to their houses, front lawns, and streets each year, and transform America into a flickering showcase of all things ho ho ho, fa la la, and Oh, come all ye faithful? What makes them spend tons of money and lots of time carting Christmas out of stores, attics, and basements? Why do they do it and how?

Let's shed some light on Christmas in America.

The Dreaded Fruitcake

In America the fruitcake is the laughingstock of Christmas foods. *Tonight Show* host Johnny Carson might be to blame, as he joked that there is really only one fruitcake in the world, and it's just passed from family to family. Carson is no longer alive but the fruitcake lives on.

Each January the Manitou Springs Chamber of Commerce in Colorado hosts "The Great Fruitcake Toss," in which the dried fruit and nut cake is propelled as far as possible like a track and field shot put. Eight Boeing engineers hold the event record of 1,420 feet, achieved with their Omega 380, a mock artillery piece fueled by compressed air and pumped by an exercise bike.

The Tacky Light Tour

The Tacky Light Tour in Richmond, Virginia, got its start in the late 1980s, when local radio personality Barry "Mad Dog" Gottlieb wanted to inject some color into Richmond's traditional white light approach to the holiday. The Tour has become outrageously popular. Amateur decorators clamber about their roofs and putter about their lawns each fall, hanging lights and adornments, and hoping to meet the increasingly stringent requirements to be included in the official *Richmond Times-Dispatch*'s Tacky Light list.

When the list began, a house had to be bedecked in at least ten thousand lights. Today, that number has tripled, and most participants far exceed that wattage. It is not uncommon for houses to be illuminated with one hundred thousand or more lights. Once the list is published, shortly after Thanksgiving, Richmond becomes a flurry of activity. With more than one hundred houses sporting at least thirty thousand lights, it is impossible to capture Christmas in Richmond in one night, and entire businesses—from tour guides to limousine parties—now cater to the seekers of light and tote them from sight to sight around Richmond.

Carloads of wide-eyed pilgrims, waiting their turn to take in the majesty, surround the listed houses like ants around a picnic morsel, all hoping for a taste of tacky.

The Christmas House

"Merry Christmas, everyone!" Al Thompson shouts, as he climbs onto a bus outside his house on Wendhurst Drive. His audience, fifty or so elderly folk from a retirement home, greet him with applause like raucous fans at a pep rally. Al's house has become a must-see stop on the Tacky Light Tour, and Al has become a much-adored cheerleader of Christmas.

"Welcome to the Thompsons'!" he continues, taking to the microphone. "You're looking at the wonder of one hundred seventy thousand lights." The crowd has overtaken the bright side of the bus, their wrinkled faces pressed flat against the windows. "There are one hundred fifty homemade items, all hand-painted. It takes four hundred hours to put it up, one hundred fifty hours to take it down. There are more than four hundred twenty-five extension cords that connect to eighty plugs, running to forty breakers in three breaker boxes, juiced by a four-hundred-amp service." Al flashes a mustached grin, while his display twinkles in his yard across the street. "Now, what else do you want to know? Anyone have any questions?"

It is both unusual and delightful to see elderly people wave their hands in the air like schoolchildren with the right answer. "When do you start decorating?" a seemingly frail woman belts out from the back, not waiting to be called on.

"I never stop," Al laughs. "Just as soon as I get them all packed away around early February, I pull out my notebook to begin plans for the next year."

"How much does it cost?"

"I try not to even think about it," Al admits. "But let's just say I try to hit the after-Christmas sales."

"Where do you keep everything?"

"Believe it or not," Al chuckles, "it all goes in labeled boxes and into the eaves of our house. There's a crawl space off the dormer windows. When you have this much stuff, you have to be pretty organized."

Al has his Christmas extravaganza figured out down to the last bulb and decorated to the last square inch. From the apex of his roof to the tiptoe edge of the curb, Al's house is a Christmas vision to behold. And this night, like every other night between Thanksgiving and New Year's Eve, Al has come home from his day job as a propane salesman and, after kissing his wife Esther hello, has headed outside for his nighttime enjoyment of greeting the throngs of onlookers who make his home a Christmas destination.

Al's journey to making the list and creating his own 170,000-light spectacular started on one such limousine tour he'd take each year with friends. While everyone else was oohing and aahing, Al was dissecting what was required to put on one of these Christmas extravaganzas. Compared to these masterpieces, Al and Esther's house was conventionally decorated at the time. There were a few lights on the bushes and a wreath on the door, but that was it.

But in 2003, Al and Esther took the tour nine nights in a row, seeing every house that was listed on every list in the area. On the ninth night, in the far-flung northeast reaches of Richmond in a suburb called Mechanicsville, Al turned onto Little Sorrel Drive. He drove past mostly understated houses with single strands of lights draped across their porches like pearl necklaces. Then he turned the corner, and, according to him, said to Esther, "Oh, my God! I want my house to look like that!"

What he saw was a house right at the end of the cul-de-sac, beaming like a movie star on opening night. The roof was outlined in lights, the windows were outlined in lights, and the yard was blooming Christmas. In Al's mind, "it popped." He got out of the car and rushed over to the driveway of Chuck and Sherry Hudgins.

Hear Ye! Hear Ye!

Since there is no mention of a "Christmas" celebration in the Bible, Massachusetts Bay Law of 1659 imposed a five-shilling fine (the equivalent of one or two days' wages) on anyone who was "found observing any such day of Christmas or the like by forgoing of labor, feasting or any other way." The law was repealed in 1681.

Chuck and Sherry Hudgins spend most nights between Thanksgiving and New Year's in their driveway, greeting guests, answering questions, and wrangling their grandchildren, who often dress as elves and hand out candy. And that's where Al found them.

"What does it take to do this?" he asked.

"You have to get your electric right," Chuck told him. "Your normal box isn't going to do it. And putting it up takes a long time, costs a lot of money, and isn't easy. So you have to be committed."

"But," Al remembers, "he also said 'it's a lot of fun.'"

That night, after talking to Chuck for an hour, Al headed home with a flicker in his eye and one question on his mind: "Can I pull this off and make it look good?" For all of 2004, Al designed, schemed, built, and shopped, determined to become "that Christmas House," the house kids remember when they grow up as being the most spectacular. He searched the Internet and looked in book after book to find the best Christmas images, driven by the challenge of whether he could then bring that vision to life.

Al has always loved Christmas. He fondly recalls the family drive each December in his dad's sedan to the "Christmas house" of his childhood in Memphis. "When my wife and I drive through Memphis and we pass that house, I turn to her and she always says, 'I know, I know. That's the Christmas house.'" Maybe that's where all of this really got started. A beacon of Christmas then, the house is comfortably inscribed in his memory now as part of "the good old days."

As the summer turned to fall of 2004, the year Al "went big," he raced to his unmovable deadline and sizable goal to have forty thousand lights on his house in order to make the newspaper's Tacky Light list. When the lights went ablaze that year, he had more than doubled his goal and his name made the paper. That first night, a line of cars began to drive

There's nothing sadder in this world than to awake Christmas morning and not be a child.

—Erma Bombeck, *I Lost Everything in the Post-Natal Depression,* 1973

slowly down his street. Al remembers looking out the window, and to his surprise he saw that a crowd had gathered.

He walked outside through the lighted tunnel and down his driveway, beneath the canopy of lights he'd created, and heard adults and children alike excitedly saying, "Look at that! Look over there." He stood before a crowd of joyous, well-lit faces. If not a turning point in his life, this was certainly a point of no return. He and his house would be forever dedicated to Christmas.

Al could not have foreseen the "human side" of creating his light display—that so many families would make his house part of their holiday tradition; nor did he realize how the love of doing it would have such a strong hold on him. But it did.

Welcome to Dasher, Georgia

According to American FactFinder, the population of Christmas, Florida, is 1,162. Other places whose names are associated with the holiday season include North Pole, Alaska (population 1,778); Santa Claus, Indiana (2,283); Santa Claus, Georgia (242); Noel, Montana (1,515); Rudolph, Wisconsin (422); Snowflake, Arizona (4,958); Dasher, Georgia (807); and at least a dozen places named Holly, including Holly Springs, Mississippi, Holly Hill, South Carolina, and Mount Holly, North Carolina.

He began his own tradition. After Al turns off the lights each night, he captures his memories in a diary, chronicling the comments of his visitors and some particularly joyful moments. One year, a few nights before Christmas, some exchange students from China visited his house. "You could tell these were brilliant people," he wrote. "Two young ladies and a young man were with their professor from Virginia Commonwealth University."

Al recalled that while the girls were off taking pictures, the Chinese man came over to him and admitted he had never seen anything quite like Al's yard. "Why?" the man asked. "Why do you do this?" Al asked him if he knew about the Christian religion. "I know that it's Jesus' birthday," the young man told him. "And that you guys celebrate that and give gifts because of the gifts from the Wise Men. But why all the

rest?" He pointed around the yard at the assortment of iconic Christmas characters. "Why that guy?" he asked, pointing at Al's snowman.

"Since Christmas is in December," Al explained, "and in some places in America we get snow, we associate snow with Christmas. Snow is friendly and snowmen are friendly. Christmas is friendly." Al's Chinese friend looked even more confused.

"Then what's the mean green thing?" he asked, tilting his head toward the giant snarling Grinch standing in Al's yard, holding the countdown calendar to Christmas. "How does that tie in?"

"The Grinch tried to steal Christmas," Al explained.

"Steal Christmas? How do you steal Christmas?"

"Good question," Al answered. "He's a fictional character who was envious of his neighbors' happiness and, in an attempt to prevent Christmas from coming, stole all their presents and decorations from them."

"Whose?"

"Yeah, the Whos. That was the family's name. But in the end, when Christmas still came and the Whos were happy anyway, the Grinch's heart grew three times its size and he gave all the presents back." His visitor looked at him. Both men were quiet. "Well," Al finished, "I probably can't explain it all to you in one night. You might want to rent the DVD."

Each year Al finds inspiration for new figures and homemade items in a variety of ways—from current movies to wrapping paper. He built his gingerbread men based on figures on a wrapped present he received. He saved the paper, then later sketched the men in his design notebook, cut out the pattern on plywood, painted them, drilled holes, and stuck the lights through. Since he began his Christmas quest, he's built twenty or thirty more each year—all meticulously drawn out in his design notebook, then brought to life in wood, paint, and lights, and deck-tested during summer trial runs with neighbors sitting outside with their beverages and acting as discerning judges.

His newest plan is to build Santa in a futuristic sled and a team of reindeer shooting through the night on the right side of his house. "The reindeer will be three feet long each," he explains. "It'll be fourteen feet all together and will be all in lights." His imagination leaps off the page. "The sleigh reminds you of a bobsled, real jazzy looking and modernistic. Santa's hat is flying behind him, very streamlined." Al stops and sighs a contented sigh. "This is what I love—figuring it all out. How am I going to get that thirty feet up in the air? How do I get it to another tree that's eighteen feet away? I've got a rope technique devised." He'll cantilever it up one end, then the other, like drunken window washers on a skyscraper. "Once I figured that out, boy was I excited!"

The morning after Christmas, Al's plans for next year are officially set in motion when he, like many Christmas megawatters, is one

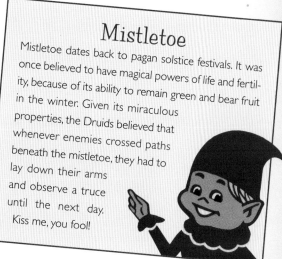

Mistletoe

Mistletoe dates back to pagan solstice festivals. It was once believed to have magical powers of life and fertility, because of its ability to remain green and bear fruit in the winter. Given its miraculous properties, the Druids believed that whenever enemies crossed paths beneath the mistletoe, they had to lay down their arms and observe a truce until the next day. Kiss me, you fool!

Christmas Traditions

When asked about childhood memories, nine out of ten adults recount a family Christmas tradition as one of their favorites. Here is some kindling to help you add a memorable spark to your Christmas.

- Make an adventure of cutting your own Christmas tree. Or get a live tree and plant it after Christmas.
- Take a Christmas Eve drive to look at lights and decorations.
- Bedeck the house to become one of the spectacles everyone drives to see.
- Give a yearly ornament marked with the date.
- Have each family member give something to someone in need.
- Read a Christmas bedtime story every night in December.
- Have a Christmas Eve picnic on a blanket placed by the tree. Let everyone open one present.
- Take a yearly photo of you and yours wearing Santa hats or reindeer ears.
- Bake cookies and leave Santa a plate of them along with a handwritten note (that can be saved).
- Hide a pickle ornament on the tree Christmas morning. The first one to find it gets a special present.

of the first in line to take advantage of the 50-percent-off sales. This past year, in a spirited burst of post-Christmas craziness, he bought forty thousand new lights and six thousand candy canes. "I gave away five thousand," he calculated. "So I told the manager of my favorite store: 'I'll take all the candy canes off your hands for seventy-five percent off.'" He packed them in his car—floorboard to ceiling—and went on his merry way. He had a lot of work to do. There were only 364 days left until Christmas.

FDNY 343

Richmond firefighter Mark Dabrishus and his wife, Michelle, and their children, Jenna, Krista, and Andrew, have long been fans of the Tacky Light Tour. When the children were young, the family started joining friends to view the Christmas lights.

"It's a tradition," Michelle said. "Before we got a bigger car we used to have to borrow a van so we could all fit inside, and every year we'd ride around Richmond. The children have always looked forward to the adventure."

From the beginning of their marriage, Mark and Michelle agreed they'd make their house memorable for their children at Christmas. "We wanted our kids to remember Christmas in their own house," Michelle explained.

"We wanted them to wake up in their own rooms, not on the road with all the presents in the car, shuttling back and forth between grandparents. We wanted Christmas to really be Christmas in our house." Like many families, they attend Christmas Eve services at their church, come home, put out some cookies for Santa, and tuck the kids in bed to await his arrival.

But then came the lights.

"We all loved the lights, even when we just had the white," Mark said with a laugh. "But one year after the Tour, I got bit by the bug. I came home and looked at my boring white lights, and decided I wanted the 'wow factor.'"

The Dabrishuses' lights helped them achieve their goal of making their house the place for celebrations. "The kids love the fact our house is over the top," Michelle said. "It's not embarrassing to them at all. It's a real family thing; one of our traditions. We do it together, and their friends even come over to help."

Jack Frost at the Beach

"The Christmas Song," with its well-known opening lyric, "chestnuts roasting on an open fire," was written by Mel Tormé and Bob Wells during a heat wave in 1944. Tormé once said that he and Wells wrote the song "in an effort to stay cool by thinking cool."

"We like that it makes it a little over-the-top hodgepodge," Mark agreed. "Christmas is something to share with each other and our friends. We love everyone's contributions."

In 2001 Mark Dabrishus decided it was time to really go for it. "It was such a sad time for our country," he remembered. "We all needed some Christmas." So he climbed up on the roof and spelled it out.

"A lot of people ask me what it stands for," Mark said, as he stood in his front yard beneath the glowing FDNY 343 his house shouts to the sky. "Three hundred forty-three firefighters lost their lives in New York on 9/11, and at this time of year we don't want to forget sacrifice like that."

And as for the roof of his house, the memory of those heroes will always be emblazoned in lights. It is a Christmas tribute to his fallen comrades that's far from Tacky.

The Royal Family of Richmond

Often called the Royal Family of Richmond Christmas Lights, the Phifers are legends on the tour. They've been doing tacky lights before tacky was Tacky. When Bobby Phifer was young, his parents, Rose and Earl, would take him and his sister to look at the decorated houses around Richmond each Christmas. Bobby's creativity sparked around fourteen, and he took to the front door of his family's house with a strand of lights he had bought at a garage sale.

Twenty-five years later, Bobby's light display has snaked its way around the door, over the house, through the yard, up the trees, and into the neighboring yard. But the neighbors don't mind: he is "the neighbors." He was so enthusiastic about decorating that he and his wife, Bobbie, bought the house next door when it went on the market; they moved into the house he'd grown up next to. In doing so, they doubled the family's decorating surface area and power, and acquired a very tall backyard tree.

The tree can be spotted well before arriving on the Phifers' street thanks to the warm glow it casts into the airspace around the neighborhood, and since traffic slows to a virtual standstill in a one-mile radius of their display, the tree serves as an enticing lure, a promise of payoff for patience. One by one, the occupants of cars, limos, and buses take turns paying respect to the royal family, which welcomes its public in the driveways of its two highly illuminated abodes. During the holidays, once the Phifers get home at night they know they are there to stay. Not that they mind being sealed in their yards like characters in a snow globe. They love having an audience.

"It's a lot of work," Bobby said. "But when you see the kids' faces, it makes it all worth it." Bobby,

Rudolph, The Red-Nosed Reindeer

Red-nosed Rudolph was created in 1938 by Robert L. May, a copywriter for the Montgomery Ward department store. He was asked to write a children's story as a gift to the store's customers, but company higher-ups were wary of the character's red nose. Caricatures at the time always depicted drunks with a red nose.

Once they saw pictures of Rudolph, the executives changed their minds. The store distributed 2.4 million copies of the story in the first year alone. A few years later, May's brother-in-law, Johnny Marks, wrote the lyrics and melody for a Rudolph song. First recorded by Gene Autry in 1949, it has since become one of the best-selling songs of all time.

In 1964 NBC aired a stop-motion animated TV special *Rudolph, the Red-Nosed Reindeer*, narrated by Burl Ives, the voice of Sam the Snowman. He tells the story of a reindeer with a red nose that lights up, whose father is so embarrassed by his son's difference that he covers the nose with mud to hide it. Rudolph's misfit nose is, of course, called upon one foggy Christmas Eve to help guide the sleigh around the world, and his name is shouted with glee. And "animagic" Rudolph, the longest consecutively running TV special, goes down in his-sto-reeeeeeeee.

who works in construction, takes to the trees each year—both in his mother's yard and now in his yard next door—perched atop a sixty-foot cherry picker. By his count, each of the big trees has more than fifteen thousand miniature lights. Comparatively, the average Christmas tree tops out at around three hundred lights, so imagine the frustration of looking for the loose bulb on a hundred Christmas trees while leaning precariously off a lift bucket sixty feet in the air.

During decorating season, while Bobby tends to the lights on high, his wife works on toting out twenty-five years of Christmas, his mother organizes her vast holiday doll collection, his children line the sidewalks with candy canes, and his sister, Deborah Carter, stakes countless homemade plywood cartoon characters into the two front yards. In 2006, when Deborah's and Bobby's father passed away, the lights almost went dim. But Bobbie said, "We couldn't do that to Rose. She wanted them on because she knew he'd want them on."

"He loved the lights," Rose said. "He loved decorating, and he loved all the people who came by over the years. I can't imagine not doing it." Bobby decided to carry on the efforts as a tribute to his father, a neighborly family tradition that Richmond would certainly be a lot darker without.

While there, I overheard a man say, "Something must be in the water. These two are definitely on a mission to one-up each other." I almost told him that it's not in the water, it's in the genes, but decided I'd let him discover the family roots beneath the great big tree for himself.

Programming Christmas

If you own a computer you've probably seen the dancing light show that was emailed and "YouTubed" to every desktop in America: a Christmas display created by Carson Williams of Mason, Ohio, who had synchronized the Christmas lights all over his yard and on the front of his house to dance to Trans-Siberian Orchestra's "Wizard in Winter."

The show was so magical and so impressive it led to a Miller Lite beer commercial, several national television appearances, and thousands of people flocking to Williams's home on a cul-de-sac. Carson pulled the plug on his show after bumper-to-bumper traffic prevented police from getting to a minor fender bender. He moved his display to a town park where, like patrons at a drive-in movie, fifty carloads at a time can sit and watch his fifteen-minute light show and listen to its soundtrack on their car radios. The display—which includes two wooden replicas of his home's facade—used eighteen hundred feet of lumber, thirty-five hundred feet of cable, and cost $192,000 to produce.

Inspired or perhaps challenged by Carson's technological wonder, hundreds of techies have followed suit, including Richmond's Ralph Shuler. When I arrived at Ralph's house, it was as devoid of Christmas lights as most of the other houses on the street. I got out of the car and walked over to the mailbox to check the street address.

Just as I approached the yard, the opening notes of "Wizards in Winter" rang out, momentarily making me think I had tripped an alarm. Lights began to dance and chase one another around the yard. It was a sight to behold—a giant real tree, a small forest of artificial trees, a herd of plastic reindeer, and other Christmas legends boogieing about the lawn to the syncopated cadence. I moved back across the street and took in the performance with a man who had a delighted little girl perched on his shoulders.

After the show I made note of the lightning bolt on the High Voltage: DO NOT ENTER sign that stood at the entry to the walkway; I called out a hello. Then Porky Pig's stammering rendition of "Blue Christmas" b-b-b-began, drowning out any hope of my being heard. During the b-b-b-blue performance, a woman walked toward Ralph's walkway, ignored the high-voltage sign, and proceeded toward the front door.

"Hi," I hollered above stuttering Porky. "Is this your house?"

Within minutes, I was sitting in Ralph Shuler and Ann Hatcher's living room, surrounded by Ann's zoo of Beanie Babies and cat collectibles, and waiting for their house's upcoming appearance on the local CBS affiliate's newscast. The two of them were like beaming, proud parents when their house flashed on the screen during the weather. I applauded. It was a neat occasion to witness.

Ralph's light odyssey began twenty years ago when his youngest son was ten. "The lights were like magic to him," Ralph explained. So he loaded the big tree out front with 175 multicolored C-7 bulbs and made his son happy. The following year, when he doubled that number, he ran out of power and spent that summer upgrading his electrical system in order to be able to double the lights for the next season. Ralph's yearly twofold pursuit has led to a ninety-thousand-bulb synchronized display that took two years to program. But the recently retired computer programmer likes seeing what he can make a computer do.

During the eight weeks leading up to Christmas, he spends eight hours a day seven days a week choreographing every note of his display. Ralph considers this a great programming challenge. He recites the names of synchronization pioneers—Mike Zminksy, Marty Slack, Carson Williams, Chuck Smith—as if they were heroes. He's particularly fond of Chuck Smith, founder of planetchristmas.com, who established a chat room where "any question you can possibly have about how to do this stuff is answered."

While most homegrown animated displays in the country have sixty-four channels of computer control, Ralph's display has double that number. His basement looks similar to NASA's launch operations center. There are numerous computers, blinking monitors, wires, dials, and knobs, and over one hundred extension cords.

"The hardest part is picking the music," he told me. "There are more than ten thousand Christmas songs, and you want something for everyone's tastes—something for the kids, something for country lovers, something for jazz people." After he picked the songs for his program, he burned a CD and listened to it over and over again that summer. Everywhere he went he was playing Christmas songs.

Unlike other Christmas lighters, Ralph has to rely on others to help him get his lights in place. "I can't climb a ladder," he said. "I have ankylosing spondylitis. It's very painful for me to walk more than thirty or forty feet at a time." Even though his hips and back are stiffening with time, he approaches his medical situation with a positive attitude and fresh ideas. Ann does most of the hanging, and this past year, during the hottest week of the summer, he wrote a letter to twenty-five neighbors and asked for help. Sixteen people volunteered, including his next-door neighbor and a teenager from down the street who helped dismantle the display.

After this year's resounding success and great reception, he's planning to double next year's display with more circuits, more songs, more channels, and, of course, more lights. The day after Christmas he was at Home Depot and Lowe's first thing buying thousands of additional lights. "Just wait and see," he pledged. "You have to come back next year because I have a few surprises up my sleeve."

The Enlightener
planetchristmas.com

Planetchristmas.com, the best spot on the Internet to get Christmas light how-tos, actually got its start thanks to an abandoned coffee vending machine. Webmaster Chuck Smith found it more than three decades ago when he was a freshman in college. The engineering major took the contraption apart and found a little mechanical computer that enabled the machine to spit out the cups of coffee, putting in the appropriate amount of sugar and cream; by Christmas he had reprogrammed the computer to sequence the lights on the bushes in front of his parents' house. "That thing was noisy," he remembered. "It was open relays jumping across arcs and you could smell the ozone."

Chuck has always loved Christmas lights. He bought his first set of fifteen for three dollars at the Rexall Drugs when he was seven years old. The strand lasted him for more than ten years, and it was a harbinger of his future dream: becoming America's preeminent Christmas lighting expert. He set up the planetchristmas.com Web site just as the Internet was starting to take off "for pretty selfish reasons"—he was tired of explaining how he made his Christmas lights dance. The site got lots of hits and today there are hundreds of thousands of enthusiasts sharing their know-how. The site is the place to go to learn how to computerize lights; to find out where you can buy everything from animatronics to light controllers, Santa suits and nativity scenes; and to talk with others who love all things Christmas.

"Everyone remembers that one house that really went all out for Christmas," Chuck said. "If you want to be that house, PlanetChristmas is here to help." Surprisingly, in this day of commercialism and buck-making, the site does not sell anything. This community of enthusiasts just wants to help others light up America.

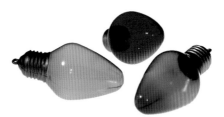

Make a Wish

Chuck and Sherry Hudgins's Christmas encrustation began the first year they started dating. Chuck asked Sherry if she'd mind if he put up a "few lights" on her house. Always a fan of Christmas, Sherry agreed and was surprised when a "few lights" turned out to be ten thousand. After that first Christmas together, their dates focused on finding additional lighted decorations to fill the dark space in the yard.

"He's got it bad," Sherry stated with a laugh.

"Everyday life is hard for most people," Chuck said, as we stood in his driveway next to the candy cane light fence. "People have come up to us and said stuff like, 'these are depressing times' and that our house has 'changed their perspective.' Or they were feeling blue and decided to go out and look at the lights, and that it gave them an 'uplifting feeling.' Everybody thanks us and appreciates what we do, and tells us how it makes them happy.

"This Christmas was kind of rough on me. I lost my mom right after Christmas last year, and she always loved the lights. One of the main things—my main memories from childhood—was riding around looking at the lights. We loved it." He took a breath and paused. "I knew having Christmas up without her would be tough, but I also knew in my heart that she'd be looking down and expecting it."

Immediately following his mother's death, Chuck began "working on Christmas," which helped him get through his loss. Working on Christmas is perhaps when he is the happiest (watching NASCAR ranks up there too). Chuck takes to the first as an artist, the second as a fan.

"He'll take an idea and run with it," Sherry said. "Like the carousel. After he got the idea to do a carousel, he had to figure out how to make it work."

Everything he could think of to make it spin—like a ceiling-fan motor—was going to make it go too fast, until he noticed their Christmas tree revolving on its rotating tree stand. It was an "aha!" moment. He drew the horses so that, like a carousel, they would go counterclockwise; he painted them, and affixed them to a plastic lawn table, which he figured was lightweight enough to be the base. He got a piece of PVC for the core and an umbrella for the top, and stuck it all together on top of the Christmas tree stand. He plugged it in, but the horses galloped backward. "Who knew that Christmas tree stands turn clockwise?" Chuck laughed.

"He asked me if they could go backward," Sherry recalled. "And I promptly said, 'No!'"

After calling the manufacturer to ask if there was a way to make it go the other way and learning there wasn't, he called a few electricians to ask if he could reverse the polarity. They all said no. He repainted the horses to match on the flipside.

"He got it pretty close," Sherry noted. "And it looks better anyway since you can see both sides as it spins around."

Chuck's work has a legion of fans and repeat visitors. Shortly after the final traces of daylight gave in to the darkness of night, a mother

pushing a little girl in a stroller came down the street. Hoofing across the cul-de-sac in her sneakers, the woman was breathing heavily. "The reindeer are still there!" the little girl shouted, pointing to the air rights between Chuck and Sherry's house and that of their neighbor.

Their new neighbors have allowed them to continue using the eye-hook in the peak of their house, installed by their old neighbors, Mike and Vickie, so that the reindeer can fly between the two houses. Vickie was very protective of Chuck and Sherry when prospective buyers came to look at their house. She always brought up Christmas, not wanting Grinches to move in.

All the Hudgins's neighbors on the otherwise relatively subdued street have been supportive. In fact, their neighborhood seems to salute the hours of work Chuck and Sherry put into their display. Some nights the neighbors gather in one of their driveways around a fire pot, watching and waving to the traffic while roasting marshmallows. There's even a rumor that the neighbors up the street are working on a plan to line candy cane lights down the road to the Hudgins's house.

The little girl from the stroller walked over to the driveway to put her "Dear Santa" letter into their mailbox and a couple of dollars into the Make-A-Wish mailbox—each year they collect more than one thousand dollars for the charity—then turned and asked Chuck, "Is Santa coming by tonight?"

"I don't think so," he told her. Seeing her frown, he added, "Well, he didn't tell me he was. But he did say he might try to stop by on Friday night." Satisfied with that answer, the little girl got back in her stroller.

"Well, I guess we'll see you Friday night," her mother said.

"He said he'd be here about six o'clock," Chuck told her with a wink. Like Superman and Clark Kent, Chuck and Santa aren't ever seen in the same place at the same time, but no one seems to notice. Or mind. Both try to make wishes come true.

1026

Ho! Ho! Homes!

Each day from Thanksgiving until Christmas, the *Durham Herald-Sun* newspaper in North Carolina runs a photo of a decorated home with a map to help people find all the local Santas, trees, elves, and houses dripping in lights. Then, around Christmas Day, the paper runs a souvenir spread of all the homes nominated as must-sees by the community.

The annual list is one of the paper's most popular features. It started out in 1994 almost as a joke, when columnist Jon Ham wanted to take his kids to look at the mega-decorated homes in the area but didn't

know where to go. "We need a map showing where these things are," he announced during an editorial meeting. "We can take nominations from the community and call the feature 'Ho! Ho! Homes!.'" Everyone groaned. And it's been an overwhelming success ever since.

Simple Elegance

A friend who teaches at Duke University in Durham told me about a beautiful Ho! Ho! Home near campus that I should see—not because of its outrageousness but because of its elegance. After the high-amp intensity of Richmond, spectacular on a more demure scale had its appeal.

When I called John Bloedorn to ask about the decorations adorning his house, he told me, "It's sort of simple, really; nothing fancy. We're actually pretty subdued, but you're welcome to come look. We just hope you won't be disappointed."

While certainly more understated than the megawatt displays of Richmond, the house was gorgeously decorated: genteel, stylish, and stunning. John and partner, Keith Wenger, owners of a Durham framing shop and art gallery, show how colored lights can be used to graceful effect. Though not caked in Christmas, their house makes a statement and demonstrates how ingeniously simple can be as visually satisfying as outrageously difficult.

"We try to have fun without smothering the house too much," Keith noted. The historic house, built in 1919 by an American Tobacco Company executive, was designed by Durham architecture firm Rose and Rose, which also worked on many of the area's churches. Since purchasing the house in 1998, John and Keith have decorated for Christmas to highlight and complement their home's good bones and fine features. Their adornments have evolved from simple white lights to colored lights and wreaths. No matter how simple it looks, don't think it means that every inch isn't well designed and perfectly studied.

"Wait!" John said, as the photo was about to be snapped. "Give me a second." He rushed into the house then came back out, running over to one of the yard's multicolored shrubs. Among the hundreds of C-7 lights on the bushes, he'd noticed a single burnt bulb. He quickly took action to replace it, proving that whether decorating with one strand or a thousand, Christmas is about taking the time to notice. And that makes it picture perfect.

Santa School

The Charles W. Howard Santa Claus School in Midland, Michigan, is a non-profit organization that was established in 1937 "to uphold the traditions and preserve the history of Santa Claus" and to provide students with the resources that allow them to "define and improve their presentations of Santa Claus." It is the longest continuously running Santa Claus school in the world.

Simple Wonder

En route through Durham, a house caught my eye. I pulled off the road and parked in the driveway. The house was quite pretty in a picture postcard sort of way yet full of spirit.

Wanting permission to take a few photographs and to learn about the hows and whys behind its decor, I walked up to the door. Just as I was about to knock, I could hear a fight. Through the giant picture window I could see a couple standing by a partially lit Christmas tree. "We fight and we fight and we @*!%#$@! fight!" the man screamed at the woman. "Why did you have to do it? You know you do the lights wrong! If I've told you once, I've told you a thousand times, you've got to go in and out, not lasso the thing!"

I quickly backed away from the door, turned, and hightailed it to the car. A fight over lights is not something I want to witness. No matter how pretty the tree turns out, it leaves an indelible, ugly impression.

As I was driving away, a house down the street caught my eye. It too was fairly simple, having a certain uncomplicated style. I stopped the car and got out, debating whether I dared walk on the lawn to photograph an adorable train (I considered my last misadventure). A woman came out of the house in a rush. "Hi," she said, dashing toward her car. "I'm Cookie. Cookie Frederick."

He errors who thinks Santa enters through the chimney. Santa enters through the heart.

—Charles W. Howard, founder, Charles W. Howard
Santa Claus School, Midland, Michigan

"Is it okay if I take some pictures?" I asked.

"Sure," she said. "I've got to run to work, but my husband will be home soon."

No sooner had the taillights of her car disappeared than a set of head-lights made its way down the street. The car pulled into the driveway and a man got out. I waved sheepishly. "Cookie said it would be okay if I took some pictures of the decorations."

"Sure," he said. "I'm her husband, John. Make yourself at home." He disappeared into the house.

He soon reappeared. "You like Christmas lights?" he asked.

"I love them," I nodded.

"Well, then you have to see my favorite house," he said. "Why don't you follow me."

About ten minutes later, we were turning our cars onto a nearby street. I immediately spotted a house so covered in Christmas lights it seemed there wasn't a dark square inch. I got out of the car and walked over to John. "Wow," I said in obvious awe. "Thanks!"

"I knew if you liked Christmas lights you had to see this house," he said. "We come here every Christmas Eve after church. It's our tradition. It was my tradition when I was a child. We'd go around and look at the Christmas lights because my mom didn't like putting lights on our house. One of the happiest Christmases of my life was the year my mom let us put some white lights on our dogwood tree and a string of red lights over our front door. Other than that, we only had blue candles in the windows.

"I vowed as an adult that that was going to change, and I married a wife who was very supportive of that. In fact, our first date was right before Christmas, and I told her how much I loved Christmas lights, particularly blue ones. When I went to pick her up for our second date, she had put blue candles in her window. I knew she was the one."

"I love the little train in front of your house," I told him.

"I got that at the hardware store for half off after Christmas a few years ago," he said. "When our house was one of the Ho! Ho! Homes!, that was what they showed. I think my congregation nominated me. But this house is always in there."

"Wait a minute," I said. "Your congregation? Are you a minister?"

"Yep," John smiled. "I'm pastor of the Yates Baptist Church. I've been a minister all my life."

"Well, then," I said. "How do *you* define the meaning of Christmas?"

"That's an interesting question," he answered. "I grew up in the Church, so the spirituality of Christmas is of course a big part of it—the story of the birth of Christ. But the lights and decorations of Christmas I think evoke the wonder of life, a magical feeling that is hard to describe, but you know it when you feel it. We don't get to feel that much as adults, and I think we miss it. Children recognize and appreciate it a little easier. But we all want to feel that magic, the feeling that these kinds of displays give. They make us awestruck."

I nodded, thanked him, and we said good-bye. I turned and stared at the house aglow across the street.

Simple Happiness

"I hope you brought your suntan lotion," Jerry Winegarden said as I walked toward his simple manger scene backed by a house blanketed in a quilt of lights.

"I have one question," I said, looking at his house.

"Let me guess," he countered. "How much is my electric bill?" I shook my head. "How long does it take?" Again, I shook my head. "How many lights are there?"

"No," I said. "I want to know why you go to all the trouble to do this."

He paused for a second, as if contemplating whether he could trust me with the answer. "It's simple, really," he said. "Some bad things happened to my family and me. Some pretty bad things. And I said, 'I'm not giving up. We may be at our darkest hour, but we've been given life and we're going to celebrate that.' I started putting lights on the house, and it made us feel better. I figured if I was going to do it, I might as well really do it. It makes us happy, and we hope it brings a little light to the world."

Amen.

Pink Flamingos and Candy Cane Trees

I read about Susan Boggs's artistic creation in the *Raleigh News & Observer* and put her vision on my list of must-sees. Hoping to get on television, Susan and her husband Arnie created a display of pink flamingos—a Santa flamingo in a sleigh riding across the lawn behind flamingos Dasher, Dancer, Prancer, Vixen, Comet, Cupid, Donner, and Blitzen. And led, of course, by the most famous pink flamingo of all—the red-nosed one not initially a part of Clement Clarke Moore's classic.

When I finally made it to the other side of the world from Durham, often called Raleigh, it was sometime after 10:30 PM. All was dark on flamingo street save for one lone streetlight, which showed the unmistakable outline of nine reindeer flamingos standing at the ready on the lawn. Christmas had gone to bed.

The house behind the flamingos was dark, except for the blue flickering light of a television in an upstairs window. Next door—home to the self-described "fairy tale utopia dreamland" of Geoffrey and Allison Williams's candy cane trees, which I had also read about in the newspaper—things looked slightly more awake. Two lights were on upstairs. Figuring this was likely my only opportunity to see candy cane trees and a pink flamingo Santa, I brazenly knocked on Geoffrey and Allison's door. A dog barked in the backyard, and I heard footsteps coming down the stairs. A man in his underwear opened the door. "I was hoping to photograph your candy cane trees," I said. "And your neighbors' flamingos."

"Oh," the man replied, as if this late-night intrusion was perfectly normal. "Give me a minute."

Seconds later his yard began to come to life—first the candy cane trees, then the giant Christmas tree created by strings of lights suspended high above the house. When Geoffrey joined me outside he explained that the method for hanging the giant tree of lights came from an old trick campers use to suspend food so bears can't get at it. He tied a hammer on one end of a rope and flung it up into the sky. "After ten or fifteen throws," Geoffrey laughed, "I nailed the limb perfectly."

Allison soon joined us. She was very concerned. "I called next door and no one answered," she reported. Every light in the house

The Manger Stays!

Television network executives did not want to have Linus reciting the story of the birth of Christ in *A Charlie Brown Christmas*, assuming that viewers would not want to sit through the reading of passages of the Bible. Charles Schultz was adamant and asked, "If we don't tell the true meaning of Christmas, who will?"

And thus Linus dropped his blanket and told Charlie Brown the story of Christmas:

"Fear not, for, behold, I bring you good tidings of great joy, which shall be to all people. For unto you is born this day in the city of David a Saviour, which is Christ the Lord. And this shall be a sign unto you; Ye shall find the babe wrapped in swaddling clothes, lying in a manger. And suddenly there was with the angel a multitude of the heavenly host praising God, and saying, Glory to God in the highest, and on earth peace, good will toward men."

was now off, including the once-flickering television upstairs. It seemed their pink flamingos were asleep for the night. "You have to see everything lit up," Allison said. "I'm going to wake them up."

While Allison went off to rouse the neighbors, Geoffrey told me that the plan for next year was to do a smaller tree inside of the giant one. "It'll make it a little more three-dimensional," he said. "But we're going to have to figure out our power situation. We already can't vacuum while the lights are on."

A loud knocking, and then a yelled whisper from Allison, "They aren't waking up!" She huffed, then disappeared around the back of the house. Within moments we heard the rattling of an aluminum storm door. "She's determined." How Geoffrey and Allison's relationship started could have been the premise of a sitcom. Geoffrey became a

single dad and decided to reduce his monthly expenses by converting half of his house into a rental apartment. Allison, a single mom, answered his classified ad and became Geoffrey's first tenant.

The first Christmas Geoffrey had a vision of making the pines in his front yard into spiraling candy cane trees. He spiraled the trees with red, and Allison followed behind, filling in the gaps with white. "And we've done it ever since," Geoffrey added. Allison returned with the news that her mission had been a success; we watched as a man in a robe scurried behind the flamingos and began plugging in cords. Section by section, the yard woke up. He waved, said "good night," and left us to appreciate his yard. The two houses together were quite a scene.

Every year when their decorations are ready, they pick a night and all the neighbors and their children gather in the street. "We have a little ceremony, then a dramatic countdown, and the lights come on," Geoffrey explained. "After a busy day, everyone loves it." He smiles and sighs, taking in the witty scene that the two yards create. "Christmas lights for me have always been magical. Maybe I'm just a goofball, but I love this."

Using the hushed tone of a talk-showlike confession, Allison shared their guilty pleasure: "Some nights we get in our car and drive around the block so we can come upon our house. We act surprised, and drive by real slow and ooh and gasp. We laugh and laugh and I say, 'Golly, we're freaks.'"

Gifts for Breezy and Brandi

Sun and palm trees may be the antithesis of snow-men and sleigh rides, but Floridians haul out the holly and bales of lights with as much enthusiasm as everyone else. They just do so wearing tank tops and shorts. In Florida I found two noteworthy displays that were made for daughters: one was inspired by a six-year-old's request; the other was created as an eight-year-old's memorial.

The Spectacle of Lights

The Osborne family earned national attention in 1993 when the Arkansas Supreme Court ordered them to turn off the Christmas light display at their house in Little Rock, Arkansas.

This bright tale began simply, as many displays around the country do. Jennings Osborne put up his first one thousand red lights in 1986, because his then-six-year-old daughter, Breezy, loved Christmas lights and asked for them as her Christmas present. "Each year after that it got bigger and bigger," Jennings recalled. "I'm never satisfied. I'm always chasing a dream." By 1993 the enthusiastic father had completely covered the family's twenty-thousand-square-foot mansion—and most of the airspace above it—in lights.

In addition to the more than three million lights, the extravaganza included a computerized light display, featuring a train engineered by a waving Mickey Mouse, and a three-dimensional replica of the world, which was suspended one hundred feet in the air and flashed Peace on Earth. The display could be seen from the air and from a distance of

eighty miles; it attracted people from all over the world, including television crews from as far away as Japan and Australia.

Neighbors became frustrated by the traffic caused by the thousands of people who flocked to see the spectacle each night; they filed a lawsuit claiming the display invaded their privacy and asked the courts to make the Osbornes turn it off. The Osbornes fought back. Self-made millionaire owners of a drug-testing company, Jennings and his wife Mitzi asserted their First Amendment rights, maintaining that the lights expressed their feelings for Christmas. During the court case their home was vandalized and there were threats made.

"We live on a four-lane highway," Mitzi said, still protesting. "We bought the houses on each side of us sight unseen, trying to make people happy. It basically comes down to the fact that our neighbors just don't like us." When one of the judges in the case told Mitzi she was naïve by not realizing that their display was trashing the neighborhood, Mitzi explained that she went out every night with one of the guards and picked up trash. The judge responded, "That's not what I meant by 'trashing.'"

To appease the neighbors and the Arkansas Supreme Court, the family made

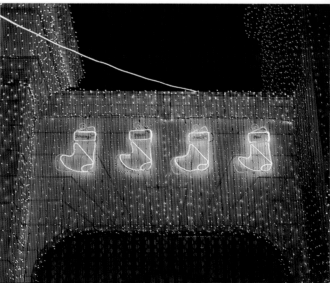

several compromises. They shortened the time the lights were on, and hired off-duty police officers to assist neighbors to get to and from their homes. But one night when a family from miles away arrived minutes after the lights were supposed to be turned off, Jennings defied the court order and turned the lights back on so that the out-of-town visitors could see them. "I just couldn't say no," Jennings remembered.

The Osbornes were fined ten thousand dollars for this transgression. "And it was worth every penny," Jennings said. But the neighbors used the act of good will to shut down the display for good.

"I thought my world would come to an end," Jennings continued. "Somebody was denying a gift I was giving."

"I've never seen my dad so crushed," Breezy remembered. "He had dreamed up most of those displays. He'd wake up in the middle of the night and write things down. Turning off the lights was just awful."

Then Disney called. In 1995 the Osbornes gave Disney World their homespun display of four million lights and eight hundred figurines, and the Osborne Family Spectacle of Lights at Disney's MGM Studios in Orlando was born. MGM transformed its New York Street, Washington Square, and Residential Street into a twinkling fantasy with everything from the Osbornes' Arkansas display, including one hundred twenty flying angels; two giant carousels; and two Christmas trees—the thirty footer with twenty-seven thousand lights and the seventy footer with fifty-eight thousand lights. According to Disney, it takes ten weeks, twenty-one thousand man-hours, seventy-one miles of extension cords, and eight hundred thousand watts of electricity to bring it to life. But it's worth it. The Spectacle of Lights remains Disney's third most popular attraction.

Not all is quiet in Arkansas, though. The Osbornes now sponsor light displays in thirty-two Arkansas cities and decorate Jimmy Carter's house in Plains, Georgia, as well as Graceland in Memphis, Tennessee. "As it turned out, it's the greatest thing that ever happened," Jennings said. "Now millions get to see it. We get to share the gift with the world."

Dear Santa Claus, How have you been? How is your wife? I am not sure what I want for Christmas this year. Sometimes it is very hard to decide. Perhaps you should send me your catalogue. —Linus, *Charlie Brown's Christmas Tales*, 2002

The Little Metal Tree

Roberta Fitzgerald's daughter Brandi was born healthy, but at three weeks of age developed spinal meningitis and went into a coma. When she awoke, she was severely handicapped, prone to seizures, and could not sit up or feed herself without help. But she loved music and lights. Every Christmas the family would snap her wheelchair into its specially designed car seat, and they'd go out to see the Christmas lights around their neighborhood of Lutz, near St. Petersburg. "She'd be at my level in the car," Roberta remembered. "I could see her smile and watch her eyes get wide as we approached the houses with lots of lights."

One night just weeks before Christmas, Roberta put eight-year-old Brandi to bed. She never woke up. After the funeral, Darrell Fitzgerald, Brandi's stepfather, impulsively took one of the triangular metal racks that had held one of the flower arrangements, wrapped it in strands of green lights, fashioned it into a little tree, and put it in their front yard.

The Fitzgeralds made the decision to decorate around that wire tree in memory of Brandi. Since then, the little green Christmas tree is warmed

by the glow of tens of thousands of lights and guarded by an army of at least twelve Santas, more than thirty snowmen, eight reindeer, and at least double the original three wise men.

This is a project that brings the Fitzgerald family together. Roberta and Darrell are assisted by their younger children, Chase and Taylor; their grown daughters, Amy and Toshia; and their grandchildren Austin, Hunter, and Jordan. "This year they slacked on me a little bit," Roberta admitted. "But we always have fun."

Roberta also works on Christmas at night. This year she re-lit all the wire animals, using plastic zip ties to secure the lights to the frames. It took her an hour per hundred lights—and she did around twenty-seven thousand lights! That's 270 hours of sitting on the floor and maneuvering reindeer and other Christmas creatures so that she could outline their wire bodies

Santa's Ordeal

According to a survey of The Amalgamated Order of Real Bearded Santas, whose many members spend each December leading up to their big night sitting on thrones at the 1,130 malls in America, Santas are sneezed on up to ten times a day; nine out of ten have their glasses yanked or beard pulled every day; and one-third of them have had to change clothes after being used as a potty.

in lights. Roberta's neck and back were kinked so badly by the end of the project that she required several visits to the chiropractor. "But," she was quick to say, "they look good don't they?"

During their almost two decades of decorating, the Fitzgeralds' memorial to their daughter has brought a lot of smiles. While we were talking in their driveway, a car drove up and parked across the street. A man helped two little girls out of the backseat, and they scampered across the cul-de-sac and stood—eyes wide, mouths agape—before the wonder of the Fitzgeralds' house.

"Daddy!" one of the girls squealed. "What's that?" She pointed to white soap flakes that sputtered out of plugged-in snowmen, fluttered in the air, and flurried onto the lawn.

"That's snow," her dad explained. "Well, Florida snow."

The man took a few pictures of the girls in front of the scene, and then walked over to Roberta. "It's beautiful," he said. "We really appreciate it. And I'm sorry for the loss of your daughter."

Roberta smiled and thanked him. He took each daughter by the hand as the girls skipped back to the car.

"I still go through it every year," Roberta admitted. "Christmas is always bittersweet. I'll never get over it, but it does help to decorate. I know she's at peace, and the lights remind me of what a lovable little girl she was. She was always full of smiles."

Westward, Ho! Ho! Ho!

Twenty-two states make up what was once known as the Wild West, the territory that lies west of the Mississippi River. When legendary pioneers carved a path westward to the Pacific Ocean, they brought Christmas traditions with them. Today's West is home to a wide frontier of twinklers, sparklers, and Kris Kringlers that can easily stand up to the light-slingers of the East. The West goes wild shortly after Thanksgiving. Lights begin to dot the landscape like fireflies in June, and the rugged terrain becomes a pageant of color.

The Trail of Lights

Exemplifying the adage that everything is big in Texas, Austin's Trail of Lights features more than 1.5 million strands of lights in a mile-long display of forty-three lighted scenes, each a unique showcase of the fantasy, magic, and make-believe of the holiday season. That's enough lights to stretch from Austin to Paris and back. But that's only the beginning of big. The Trail of Lights also features the World's Tallest Man-Made Christmas Tree.

Started in 1965 as Yule Fest, a four-day event featuring a candlelit path, a live nativity scene, and a Yule log, the Trail of Lights has become one of Texas's biggest Christmas traditions, attended by hundreds of thousands during its two-week run each December.

The brainchild of Mrs. Alden (Mabel) Davis, chairperson for Austin's Special Holiday Activities Committee, The Zilker Tree was first lit on December 10, 1967, as a way to bring attention to the city parks. The tree is hard to miss: it stands 165 feet tall and is composed of thirty-nine streamers, each holding eighty-seven multicolored, twenty-five-watt red, green, yellow, blue, and white bulbs. That's 3,543 multicolored lights beaming 88,575 watts of light into the night sky of Austin.

A team of city electricians decided to design the tree around one of Austin's Moonlight Towers. Austin was one of the first American cities to employ this modern streetlight innovation, a system of carbon arch lamps situated atop 150-foot wrought iron poles in clusters of six, and the Zilker Tree designers took advantage of that height. They circled the tower with nineteen utility poles, each fourteen feet tall, creating a base that is 120 feet in diameter and has a circumference of 380 feet. They crowned their masterpiece with a double star that measures ten feet across from point to point and is lit with 150 frosted bulbs.

Forty years later the electricians' sky-reaching design continues to serve as a holiday beacon, drawing crowds to ease on down the path of Austin's rainbow; a crew of thirty ensures that it dazzles. As in Frank L. Baum's Oz, many of the wizards work behind the stage curtain.

21 Million Christmas Trees

According to the U.S. Department of Agriculture, each year approximately twenty-one million Christmas trees are cut in America on 21,904 farms, accounting for $506 million in sales. Oregon produces 6.5 million trees a year, the most of any state (in Clackamass County alone 2.6 million trees are cut).

Austin's theatrical and artistic community supplies most of the artisans who contribute to the imaginative sound, light, and sculptural displays.

Each spring the creative team attempts to one-up the previous year's excitement, submitting renderings to the parks department and the city's Cultural Affairs division. Though the original Twelve Days of Christmas display and the massive Yule Log remain, as well as the classics like Santa's House and Silent Night, there have been updates: the toy soldiers are now multiethnic and SpongeBob SquarePants now has a spot alongside SantaSaurus and Candy Land.

The entire town seems to come out when the Parks and Recreation Department and Austin Energy hold the lighting ceremony. In 1967 then-mayor Emma Long flipped the switch on the first tree, but every year since this honor has been awarded to the young winner of a city-wide tree-coloring contest. Children are asked to create original 8½-by-11-inch interpretations of the tree; they make drawings with crayon, watercolor, and paint, or they create collages. Some of this artwork has been transformed into light sculptures and added to the trail.

Once lit, the Trail of Lights is a Technicolor playground for kids ages two to ninety-two, and the Zilker Tree is a beacon of good cheer to the city of Austin. To stand within it and look skyward is like gazing into a sparkling, colossal prism—a spiraling kaleidoscope of color and light. Many people have suggested it should be mandatory to take a spin beneath its swirling, twinkling lights. According to historian Gloria Mata Pennington, "We hear stories of how children remember twirling under the tree with a parent and how they return as grown-ups to twirl with their own children." One Zilker Tree tradition that has evolved is that couples will lock arms and spin under the tree while looking up at the lights. The result is a lightheaded vision of twinkling lights and a very dizzy feeling—both of which are good excuses to fall to the ground in a loving embrace.

A Greener Christmas with LED

The biggest Christmas "d'oh!" moment often comes after we've untangled the lights, balanced on the ladder, and gotten them perfectly in place. One bulb among the hundreds becomes dislodged, and the set mysteriously goes dark. Wiggling, pulling, and testing the line, light by light, is the only thing that can be done. It is an arduous task that often leads to cursing and fist shaking.

LED Christmas lights alleviate that problem—LED lights are illuminated by the movement of electrons and do not have a filament that can burn out or dislodge—and as an added bonus they are environmentally friendly. LED lights cut energy consumption by up to 90 percent.

The Alliance to Save Energy has done the math, and the cost saving is dramatic. A household burning ten strands of lights for eight hours a day for a month at $0.0853 per kilowatt-hour would spend $127.67 for large incandescent bulbs, $7.20 for typical minilights, and just $0.72 for LEDs.

Though they've been around for years, only recently, in this more environmentally aware time, have they started to catch on. Since the color emitted from LEDs is actually part of the light spectrum rather than the result of a colored glass placed over a clear bulb, the color is more vibrant and many think more visually exciting. Since starting his Christmas display in 1999 when he was sixteen years old, Arizonan Michael Anderson made it his goal to be completely energy efficient. His display now includes twenty-nine thousand computer-animated lights, 80 percent of which are LEDs. By next year, he's determined to "go all LED."

NOTE: The Alliance to Save Energy recommends using timers to limit light displays to no more than six evening hours a day. Leaving lights on twenty-four hours a day will quadruple your energy costs—and create four times the pollution.

Blossoms of Light

The most popular time of year for couples to get engaged is Christmas. In fact, "the question" is popped almost one million times in December. Brad Hildebrand and Jennifer Menard were among the million couples who decided to take the leap that month.

Jennifer might have known something was up when Brad asked her to buy some warm boots for their date. He tried his best to keep his motive a secret and she tried her best not to ask too many questions—like why Brad wore a backpack when the two of them went to the opening night of the annual Blossoms of Light show at the Denver Botanic Garden.

The elegant and spectacular display of one million colorful lights illuminates the plants and trees on the paths throughout the garden's twenty-three acres, creating a magical realm of romance. Around every corner and over every bridge, flora is aflame with light and color—everything from a forest of trees in autumnal hues to electric green lily pads floating atop a frozen pond. The park offers visitors special 3-D glasses, which makes the experience akin to walking inside a sparkling snow globe.

The most romantic locations within the gardens are selected by the staff; they are marked with ornate balls of mistletoe and deemed kissing spots. Each year these dozen smooching locations contribute to an average of thirty proposals, and Brad planned to be the year's first.

When Denver mayor John Hickenlooper flipped the switch, the garden burst into brilliant color, and the crowd into mitten-muffled applause. Brad grabbed Jennifer's gloved hand and took off down the big circular path, telling her to let him know when they arrived at her absolute favorite spot.

"I was nervous," he admits, "But it was also freezing cold—eight degrees—and I wanted to keep moving."

Finally, near the end of the path, beneath the twinkle of lit trees, she stopped and announced, "This is my favorite spot!" He took off the backpack and pulled out the memory book he had given her the previous Valentine's Day. In it he had put the little reminders of their journey together—from her phone number, which she'd written on the back of a Christmas card, to novelties, ticket stubs, and pictures from a few of their trips. He cleared off snow from a bench and invited her to sit with him to go through the book.

When they got to the last page, Jennifer moved to close it. "Wait," Brad said. "There's a new page." He turned to the new page in the book, which was woven with silver embroidery thread and to which he had tied an engagement ring. He got down on one knee and asked Jennifer to marry him. Her answer was yes. Darin McGregor, a photographer on assignment for the *Denver Rocky Mountain News*, witnessed the scene and caught the "kissing spot" moment on film. When he introduced himself to the couple after snapping their picture, Brad laughed and said, "Feel free to run that on the front page of the paper."

The next day all of Denver saw the news.

The Christmas Boat Parade

In 1907 an Italian gondolier named John Scarpa, who had relocated from his native country to the southern California coast, began the tradition of taking visitors on a ride across Balboa Bay in a gondola decorated with Japanese lanterns. The following year, the success of the inaugural sail led to the creation of a loosely organized Christmas parade in Newport Beach consisting of nine vessels—his gondola followed by eight Japanese-lantern-lit canoes. The parade was an immediate hit with both passengers and those along the shore.

The "Illuminated Water Parade" was held again in 1913. This time boats were judged and prizes awarded for the best-decorated and best-lit vessels. Another larger parade followed in 1914, but it was perhaps the 1915 parade on the Fourth of July that was memorably dramatic. According to Newport Beach historians, forty boats participated in the festivities, and the astonishing event featured a derelict boat hull set afire, a dramatic "rescue" of passengers, a "Battle of Fireworks" between two launches, and the explosion of two underwater mines. The dangerous celebration was witnessed by thousands of spectators, none of whom were hurt.

When World War I began, a severe depression hit Newport Harbor and the parade was not held for several years. But in 1919 Joseph Beek, developer of the Balboa Ferry Line, resurrected the parade. Every year from 1919 through 1949, with the exception of several years during World War II, the floats were constructed in Beek's garage, decorated by children, and towed around the harbor. But in 1949 city leaders decided to rein in the parade, fearing its popularity was causing too much traffic.

But one tradition wasn't sunk. Several years before, Newport Beach city employees had installed a lighted Christmas tree on a barge and towed it around the harbor while its passengers sang Christmas carols to residents on shore. Several years after the city leaders stopped the official parade, the Beeks began providing one of their ferry boats for the floating Christmas tree celebration; each year other lighted boats joined the procession. The parade came back to life.

Today more than a hundred vessels, including stunning luxury yachts, are involved. The five-night, fourteen-mile Newport Beach Christmas Boat Parade is hailed as one of the best holiday happenings in America. It attracts more than one million spectators a year, contributing millions of dollars to the local economy. There's now a system of registering boats, giving out guidebooks to participants, having marshals and parade officers, and a judged boat-decorating contest with a yearly theme, such as "Holiday Magic Through the Eyes of a Child" and "A Winter Waterland."

To sustain the level of excitement over several nights and along the fourteen-mile course, participants don't know when the judges will be there or where. The judges look for animation, creativity, and overall enthusiasm when choosing winners. And the competition is serious: some boat owners have spent more than fifty thousand dollars in pursuit of the prize.

Wednesday night's cannon boom signals the beginning of the Christmas Boat Parade. It is awe-inspiring to see the swarm of news helicopters overhead, the parade of lights launching on the water, and the throngs of people gathered along the shore waving to and cheering on the floating Christmas cards. "Today, there's a lot of negativity being shot at us in so many different ways," Richard Luehrs, president and CEO of the Newport Beach Chamber of Commerce, commented. "This is a moment in time in which everyone seems miles away from those negative stories. It's a happy escape for all of us."

Candy Cane Lane

Seattle's Candy Cane Lane (otherwise known as Park Road Northeast) is an act of community cooperation that has been a Christmas destination for more than sixty years, delighting young and old alike. For two weeks each December, this cul-de-sac is abuzz with Christmas activity as it transforms itself into Candy Cane Lane. On decorating day, a Saturday in early December, residents adorn their yards with a six-foot candy cane; one of twenty-four signs reading "peace" in different world languages; and an ample array of other Christmas-themed lawn confectionary of their choosing. At the center of this loop is a carousel, which swirls around a giant holly bush as holiday music broadcasts from one of the nearby houses.

But the origins and legacy of Candy Cane Lane are a mystery, and its legendary beginnings run as deep as the tale of Santa himself. Just how did it happen that each house came with a giant red-and-white-striped stovepipe candy cane stashed in its basement?

According to filmmaker Jamie Hook, who researched the early days of the street for the newspaper *The Stranger*, Candy Cane Lane's genesis was the handiwork of Japanese immigrant Tatsuya "Lawrence" Kawabata, who returned to Seattle in 1945 after spending almost two years at Minidoka internment camp in Idaho. He, like other Japanese-Americans, were "evacuated" from Western coastal areas at the behest of President Franklin D. Roosevelt's Executive Order 9066. However, Kawabata's spirit and patriotism were undeterred by the detainment, and he quickly reestablished himself in Seattle.

In 1949, when the government relaxed restrictions on energy consumption that had been in place since the attack on Pearl Harbor, *The Seattle Times* sponsored a city-

White Christmas

"White Christmas" is the best-selling song of all time, with more than one hundred million copies sold. It was written by Irving Berlin, who was Jewish, and originally sung by Bing Crosby in the 1942 movie *Holiday Inn*, for which it won the Academy Award for Best Original Song. Armed Forces Radio played it on April 30, 1975, as the prearranged signal for Americans to evacuate Saigon, ending the Vietnam War.

Legend has it that Berlin, who often stayed up through the night writing, told his secretary one morning, "Grab your pen and take down this song. I just wrote the best song I've ever written. Hell, I just wrote the best song that anybody's ever written!"

wide contest to see who could "best capture the spirit of Christmas through the decoration of their house." Kawabata took to the challenge in the house he'd recently purchased on Park Road Northeast. He constructed a Passion scene out of wood in the cul-de-sac facing him. Though his scene lost the contest to Oddvar Nordall's hand-carved reindeer festooned with lights, Kawabata's decorations won a lot of fans.

The following year he was more enthusiastic in his efforts. Candy canes were now being mass produced and had become the popular Christmas confection of the day. Kawabata planted large hand-painted candy canes in his lawn and began leaving baskets of real candy canes for visitors and kids in the neighborhood. Word spread and so did his display; he began using his neighbors' yards for his ever-growing scenes. By 1955 he had created a hand-painted wooden sign heralding the street, and "Candy Cane Lane" was mentioned in the *Times*.

As they say, the rest is history. Well, sort of. Several of the current residents say the whole story is a hand-me-down fairy tale. Complete hogwash. According to retired schoolteacher Barbara Reider, whose husband made the carousel around the holly bush in the 1960s using a modified airplane engine, Candy Cane Lane began because a Seattle City Light employee who lived on the street, "with the last name of Kennedy," got some

Candy Canes

The candy cane originated more than 350 years ago, when candy makers made straight, hard sugar sticks that were white. In 1670 the choirmaster at the Cologne Cathedral in Germany bent the sugar sticks into canes to represent a shepherd's staff; he gave them to children to keep them quiet during long-winded nativity services. The custom of handing out candy canes during these services spread throughout Europe and later to America.

The first reference to candy canes in America is in 1847, when German immigrant August Imgard used them to decorate the Christmas tree in his home in Wooster, Ohio. It is not certain when red-and-white-striped candy canes were made, but by 1900 they were depicted on Christmas cards.

There are many myths about candy canes. One is that candy canes were created to symbolize the purity of Jesus: the three white stripes symbolized the Holy Trinity; the red symbolized the blood Jesus shed for humankind. The shape, either that of a shepherd's staff or the letter J, both symbolized Jesus.

According to the National Confectioners Association, Americans buy 1.8 billion candy canes a year.

lights the power company was going to dispose of and put them on the street's giant holly bush in the roundabout.

Could Mr. Kennedy's light windfall have brightened what Mr. Kawabata had already started? Perhaps. Mr. Kawabata apparently moved away before any of the current residents moved in, and no one—not even the old-timers—seems to know how every house on the street comes with a hand-painted six-foot candy cane made out of very old stovepipe. Shirley Petersen, who has lived on the street for forty-five years, admits her stovepipe candy cane was in the basement when she and her husband moved in; she hadn't thought about why since. And who made the first "Candy Cane Lane" sign is also up for debate. Barbara Reider said it might be written down in the "official memory book." Just don't ask where the book is, since no one seems to remember.

But several things are certain about Candy Cane Lane. It won *The Seattle Times*'s decorating award in the 1960s, the last year it was given out, and Reider has the trophy to prove it stashed "somewhere"; each August, for more than forty years, the neighbors have held a

"Merry Christmas" Around the World

AFRIKAANS: Gesëende Kersfees

BRAZILIAN: Feliz Natal

CZECH: Prejeme Vam Vesele Vanoce a stastny Novy Rok

DANISH: Glædelig Jul

ESKIMO: Jutdlime pivdluarit ukiortame pivdluaritlo!

FINNISH: Hyvää Joulua

FRENCH: Joyeux Noël

GERMAN: Froehliche Weihnachten

GREEK: Kala Christouyenna

HAWAIIAN: Mele Kalikimaka

HEBREW: Mo-adim Lesimkha. Chena tova

IRISH: Nollaig Shona Dhuit

ITALIAN: Buon Natale or Buone Feste Natalizie

JAPANESE: Shinnen omedeto. Kurisumasu Omedeto

KOREAN: Sung Tan Chuk Ha

LATIN: Natale hilare

LITHUANIAN: Linksmu Kaledu

NAVAJO: Merry Keshmish

NORWEGIAN: God Jul

POLISH: Wesolych Swiat Bozego Narodzenia

PORTUGUESE: Feliz Natal

RUSSIAN: Srozhdestovm Kristovim

SPANISH: Feliz Navidad

SWAHILI: Kuwa na Krismasi njema

THAI: Suksun Wan Christmas

VIETNAMESE: Chuc Mung Giang Sinh

WELSH: Nadolig Llawen

communal yard sale with all proceeds going to offset expenses; and Candy Cane Lane has become a Seattle institution, which its homeowners are very protective about continuing.

The houses are decorated with unanimous participation; even "the modern house" on the street displays a candy cane. And when neighbors move out, torchbearers are sought. Just ask Heidi and Shaine Gross, who discovered that Christmas was the key to landing the house of their dreams in the competitive Seattle housing market.

They fell in love with a beautifully renovated house on Park Road Northeast. They were a little surprised when then-homeowners Bruce Ball and Dennis Worsham asked if they'd come for an interview. After some general questions, the conversation became more specific: "What do you think about Christmas?" and "What do you think of Candy Cane Lane?"

Shaine immediately enthused about Christmas, and went on to say that, though he had never been to Park Road Northeast during the holidays, they knew that it was quite a Seattle tradition—and that they were all for helping to continue it. Even though their offer wasn't the highest, their answer clinched the deal. The highest bidders had answered the question with a candy cane melting: "We'll

participate if we have to." Bruce and Dennis, loyal to the stripe, rejected a higher offer for the higher good.

When the neighbors held a going-away party for Bruce and Dennis, they invited Shaine and Heidi. Everyone was talking Christmas and asked the new couple if they had decided how they were going to decorate. "It was February," Heidi recalled. "We hadn't even thought about Christmas yet."

In addition to providing a book with everything they would need to know about their new house, Bruce and Dennis bequeathed to their

home's new owners their Grinch scene, including Cindy Lou Who and Max the dog. And given that they were told it went over really well with the kids, Shaine and Heidi decided they'd stick with that success.

During the summer, when the yearly Candy Cane Lane planning meeting was held, Shaine and Heidi slowly realized that Bruce and Dennis left some pretty big stockings to fill. Who was going to organize the fundraising garage sale? Who was going to work on the carousel?

"Bruce and Dennis's house used to have the music," someone said. "Whose house is going to have the music this year?"

When someone else quickly volunteered, Heidi thought *whew*, but said, "That's wonderful." But when the music was tested that December, it was determined that the sound was not quite as good as when it was at Bruce and Dennis's. So the music was returned to its original location.

"It wasn't so bad," Heidi said, laughing. "We put the speakers out the window and the stereo on a timer."

And the fairy-tale tradition of Candy Cane Lane played on. After all, tradition is tradition for a reason, even if no one knows who started it.

The Twelve Days of Lutherville, Maryland

The families on Barts Court aren't worried about the cost of Christmas. Their twelve days' worth of gifts—from the partridge in a pear tree to the twelve drummers drumming—are already paid for in full. In fact, they come with the houses. Since the early 1990s, the ten houses on the street have displayed hand-painted signs depicting one of the gifts presented in the popular Christmas song.

Artist Peter Mischa created a sign for each day's gift. The twelve signs are put up each year without fail, even as houses have been sold and new neighbors have moved in. The tradition is taken so seriously that displaying the signs has become a stipulation in the sale of some of the homes.

The 12 Days of Christmas on Barts Court

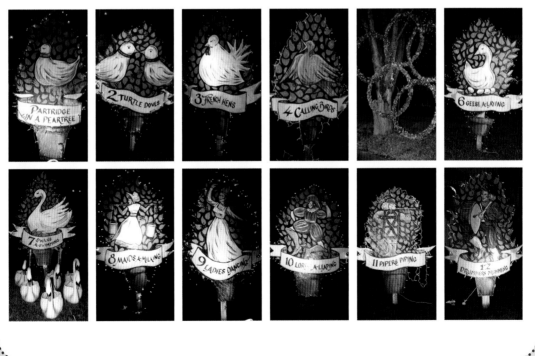

Back East

On the way home for the holidays, I decided to make two more stops: the first, in Washington, D.C., to pay a visit to our national Christmas trees, and the second, in Baltimore, because I'd heard there is a miracle on 34th Street.

In each city, hundreds of thousands of visitors make the trip to behold holiday decorating traditions: one that unites a nation, another that unites a street.

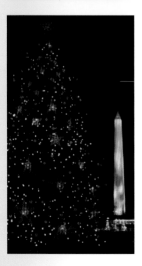

Our National Christmas Trees

The custom of having a National Christmas Tree began at 5:00 PM on Christmas Eve 1923, when President Calvin Coolidge stood outside the White House beneath a forty-eight-foot-tall balsam fir from his home state of Vermont and touched a button to illuminate twenty-five hundred red, white, and green electric bulbs.

Since then there have been many symbolic moments revolving around the lighting ceremony. In 1934 President Franklin D. Roosevelt used the occasion to suggest, "the spirit of Christmas knows no race, no creed." When President Harry Truman lit the tree in 1945 after World War II ended, it was considered a signal to light thousands of trees in communities across the country. The following year, the lighting ceremony became a televised event and by the mid-1950s, the festivities were watched by millions of television viewers and broadcast on Voice of America radio in thirty-four languages.

In 1979, when President Jimmy Carter's daughter, Amy, flipped the switch, only the top star lit. The president announced that the tree would remain dark until the American hostages in Iran were set free. The tree remained dark that year. In 1980 President Carter lit the tree for only 417 seconds, a second for each day of the Americans' captivity in Iran. When the hostages were finally released on January 20, 1981, the tree was redecorated and lit for their return.

The Capitol Tree, also known as the "People's Tree," was introduced in 1964 by then-Speaker of the House John McCormack and has been lit each year since, traditionally at 5:00 PM on December 9.

After attempts to plant a live Douglas fir on the west front lawn of the Capitol ended with dead trees, the United States Forest Service was asked for assistance. Each year since, the Capitol Christmas Tree has come from a national forest. It is decorated with ornaments created by students at an elementary school in the home state of the selected tree.

Miracle on 34th Street

Baltimore native Bob Hosier doesn't want to think about how much money he has spent on Christmas decorating over the years. And he doesn't want any money for his efforts either. He's spent "a lot" and he's been offered "a lot" but money isn't what's important to his Christmas. He decorates for the love of it—both his and everyone else's.

Bob's is the first house on 34th Street in Baltimore. His house is the anchor and light-origination point of a block-long strip of twenty-two rowhouses that becomes one of Baltimore's most unforgettable spectacles each Christmas. An estimated hundred thousand people come to 34th Street each season; they crowd the narrow sidewalks to walk, gawk, and talk about the marvel of it.

The block looks like Santa's sleigh flew in from the southwest and skidded down the rooftops, accidentally spilling the contents of Christmas

about. Anything related to Christmas—gingerbread men, elves, angelic dolls, drummer boys, candy canes—can be found in front of one of these houses, tied together with strands of lights that crisscross in swags over the street. And if it's not related to Christmas, well, someone who lives in one of the twenty-two houses might find a way to make it related, like artist Jim Pollock; he used 143 hubcaps to make a shiny eight-foot-tall post-modern Christmas tree.

Bob Hosier's inspiration came from a childhood memory. An old woman who lived in the house across the street decorated her house in an over-the-top way and played Christmas music on a Victrola on her porch.

All the kids in the neighborhood made fun of her, except Bob: he adored her house. He'd stare out his living room window at her colored lights, straining to hear the music.

At age twelve he got a job in a grocery store in northeast Baltimore. "They taught me how to cut meat," he said. "Can you believe a twelve-year-old cutting meat? By the time I was sixteen, I was a full-fledged butcher, but that's another story. The point is, I made money and bought some Christmas decorations."

The winter of his twelfth year, he, like the woman across the street, decorated his house. "My father was nervous about all the electrical cords and hot lights," Bob recalled. "But when I lit the thing up, it was like 'wow.'

I remember my parents coming out and sitting in the yard, and my dad saying, 'This is very nice.'"

Bob married into a family that loved Christmas as much as his own, and moved to the house on 34th Street where his wife, Darlene, was born. Darlene's dad had been decorating the house since 1947, so she was used to it. "Just not to my extreme," Bob chuckled. "And, yes, people laughed at me like I was the old woman across the street."

Bob went "really crazy" around 1990. Darlene came home to find that he'd re-created the homecoming scene from her favorite movie, *It's a Wonderful Life*. That's the year Lloyd O. Wolf, a neighbor known as "Mr. Lou," suggested Bob run lights from house to house. Mr. Lou had been a fan of Bob's adornments from the start. He'd always sit on his porch and watch Bob decorate, cheering him on and offering advice. Bob recalled, "The day Mr. Lou died, he had sat on his porch and watched me hanging the lights."

Once Bob swagged the lights back and forth across the street, pole-to-pole, the neighboring houses began to catch on to his lighting approach. Contrary to urban legend, there are no covenants written into real estate transactions requiring that homeowners on 34th Street take part in the pageantry. But newcomers over the years have kept the faith. People

Outdoor Lighting Like a Pro

✳ GET YOUR ELECTRIC RIGHT
Make sure you have enough amps to support your megawatt dreams. You can never have enough extension cords. Make sure they are exterior-grade. Use exterior outlets only; never run cords out of the window.

✳ TAKE AN INVENTORY
Keep a notebook of your lights, ornaments, and figures. Test all lights, replacing burned-out bulbs before you hang them. If you're buying new, "think green" and buy LED. These use 90 percent less energy and produce vivid colors.

✳ SKETCH YOUR IDEAS
Measure your yard and your home's facade, and then draw an accurate diagram of them. Decide where you want to decorate for best effect before you take to the ladder.

✳ SECURE YOUR DISPLAY
Depending on where you live, wind and weather can be brutal in December. Make sure your decorations will hold. Don't put nails, staples, or screws into your house, as the holes will enable water to get inside. Buy special clips to hold lights to your eaves or gutters, and sturdy stakes for anything in the ground.

✳ STORING ISN'T BORING
Find products that allow you to roll up strands of lights, like a garden hose holder, so that you won't greet next season with tangles. Mark all boxes using masking tape and a marker, so you know what's inside.

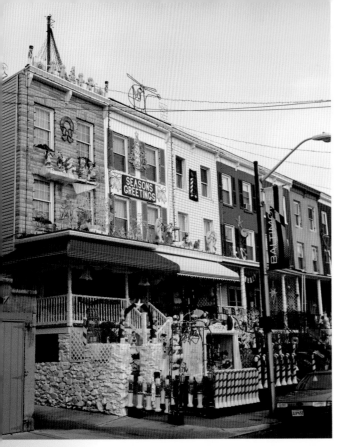

are careful to find buyers who want to carry on the tradition.

"I don't do the same thing every year," Bob explained. "Basic things, yes, but I have enough decorations to rotate stuff around and keep it fresh." Hidden in plain sight in an undisclosed location somewhere in Baltimore is a fifty-three-foot tractor-trailer filled with Bob's vast collection of Christmas decorations, including the original decorations he bought as a child. "I have enough stuff to decorate every house on this street," he said.

Most people who attend the street's spectacle are astounded by the effort involved. Many offer donations to help with the expenses, but the homeowners pool their own money to help pay for the electric bills and have made it a policy not to accept donations. "A princess from some foreign country sent me a check for several thousand dollars," Bob remembered. "And I sent it back with a note saying, if it made her feel good to write a check, please write it to a charity." He doesn't want money to get involved and mess up a good thing.

One Christmas Bob was standing on his front porch—among the collection of 140 dolls and a menorah he puts up for his friend Dave. He was dressed as an elf and handing out candy canes, and a man came up to him. The man was crying and said, "This is the prettiest thing I've ever seen." He handed Bob a one hundred dollar bill.

"I don't want any money," Bob told him.

"But you have to take it," the man said. "It's my gift."

Bob gave him his charity line, and the man nodded and walked away. A little while later, he returned and handed Bob a bottle of Dom Perignon. "I'll drink to that!" Bob said to the man.

Bob tells the generous-hearted people who appreciate his efforts, "The best gift of all would be if you take a little of this back to your neighborhood. You can't get this overnight—we're a bunch of nuts here—but if everyone went home and put a little something on the porch or a strand of lights on the house it would spread a lot of joy."

He remembers early on someone telling him that once you do it and people come, you'll always have to do it. He replied, "If I lived on a dead-end street in the desert, I'd still decorate this way." It takes six months of planning to put the whole scene up, and three months to take it down, leaving only about ninety days a year that Bob is not looking at Christmas. "It's not a problem for me," Bob said. "The point is that it makes others happy. And that makes me happy."

Christmas in New York

On my cross-country adventure I met hundreds of people who approach Christmas with wide-eyed enthusiasm, but it was on the plane back to New York that something finally occurred to me. I noticed a flight attendant's well-worn snowman pinned to her blouse as she handed me a bag of peanuts. "Oh," I said, pointing. "Your snowman lost an eye."

"He's winking," she said, without missing a beat. "It's all how you look at it."

That, I suppose, couldn't be truer about Christmas. Figuring out what the holiday means to us and how it should "look" is perhaps one of our greatest yearly challenges. We want sparkle and glitz, but decry commercialism. We want it to look hard, but be easy. We want to remember the reason for the season, yet we now have so many. We want to give, but we have to admit it's also nice to get. Simply put, we all want the perfect Christmas. Whatever that means.

Even to be an average decorator at Christmas takes a lot of effort. But to be extraordinary requires a lot of heart, tremendous patience, and more trouble than most of us care to take on. Fortunately, there are people who are willing to do "that house"—the one the rest of us can point at and be dazzled by.

Amazing Hoofers

Mathematician Christopher Whitt has calculated the following: In order for Santa to make his 91.8 million stops in the night, his sleigh must travel 650 miles per second—3,000 times the speed of sound. Wow! Those reindeer can really hoof it!

As we flew into the New York area, the ground thousands of feet below became a glowing grid of electrical wonder. Every now and then during our approach, I could see specific houses and apartment balconies burning a bit brighter than the ones around them. Those, I now realize, are where the real elves live—the people who look at Christmas with an eye toward making it magical.

Though many New Yorkers live stacked on top of one another in apartments, I've discovered during my Christmases in New York that there are people in the boroughs who take to their houses as enthusiastically as other decorators around the country.

In Brooklyn's Dyker Heights, for example, Christmas decorating has become a sport. Homeowners go to great efforts to impress the thousands of people who drive among their multimillion-dollar manses during the holiday season. Decorating businesses have been created to cater to residents who want their houses to shine without having to climb on their roofs themselves.

Enthusiastic decorating can be found on Long Island as well. Michael and Rosina Liquori of Glen Cove decorate with a passion that makes even jaded New Yorkers stop in their tracks. Their yard is filled with more than four hundred plastic blow molds and countless lights, and their street is always packed with onlookers and satellite trucks filming the spectacle for the television news. After twenty years of all-out decorating, the Liquoris have become New York legends.

And in Franklin Square, the "Christmas house" of the Culmone family—Frank, Diana, and son Christopher—has been an attraction for many years. It started with a wooden Rudolph cutout with a blinking red nose that was acquired from a bar in 1948 and placed on the side of their house. From that point, Christmas spread contagiously over their home. An artist, Christopher recently converted their garage into a scene from Rockefeller Center, an exact replica down to the Salvation Army Santa. "That was a surprise," Diana laughs. "One day I walked by and Rockefeller Center was in our garage." Never mind if they can't park the car.

Better to Give . . .

Bring some warmth to your heart during the holiday season by giving to those in need. Since choosing a meaningful charity is sometimes difficult, charitynavigator.org is an online database to provide some ideas and help you make an educated decision. Choose a charity that most fits your personal spirit of giving, whether for children, adults, pets, or other causes. Here are five ideas:

✳ TOYS FOR TOTS

Donate a new toy or give a donation to help make Christmas a little brighter for a needy child in your community. Toys for Tots collects new, unwrapped toys each year during October, November, and December, and distributes the toys as Christmas gifts to needy children in the community in which the campaign is conducted. For more information, log on to www.toysfortots.org.

✳ MY TWO FRONT TEETH

This organization offers an online gift-giving experience to aid underprivileged children. These children are selected through community organizations and allowed to individually pick their one holiday wish. Each child's wish profile is featured in an online database where donors then choose an online sponsorship. For more information, log on to www.mytwofrontteeth.org.

✳ MAKE-A-WISH FOUNDATION

Make the holiday season special by helping a child's dream come true. Make-A-Wish's unique holiday donation options help grant the wishes of children with life-threatening medical conditions. For more information, log on to www.wish.org.

✳ THE DOE FUND

The Doe Fund strives to help end homelessness for the individuals it serves by developing and implementing cost-efficient, holistic programs that meet the needs of the diverse homeless population. For more information, log on to www.doe.org.

✳ ANIMAL CHARITIES OF AMERICA

This nonprofit organization pre-screens high-quality animal-related charities and presents them for your giving consideration. The goal of the charity is to protect pets, wildlife, and endangered species, as well as the training of animals as helpmates for and companions to people in need. Log on to www.animalcharitiesofamerica.org for more information.

May Peace be your gift at Christmas and your blessing all year through!

—Anonymous

The Parade

The Christmas season has its official start each November on the Thursday morning when Santa makes his way down Broadway in Macy's annual Thanksgiving Day Parade. The parade features gigantic helium-filled character balloons tethered to earth by hundreds of handlers;

marching bands; and sparkly floats topped by lip-synching celebrities, surrounded by hundreds of human shields posing as thematically clad extras. Though I had watched the parade on TV all my life, I actually participated in it in 1990, my first Christmas in New York. I was on Broadway. Literally. And it was freezing cold and raining.

I had been hired by Macy's to dress as a British police officer and act on the eighth floor in a theme-park-style romp starring that year's featured holiday mascot: Paddington Bear. It was a ten-minute musical extravaganza featuring several basic step-ball-changes on a stage wedged between racks of little-girl tutus and shelves of infant tights. If shoppers made a purchase, they could take home a stuffed Paddington Bear as a nominally priced add-on.

Besides the hourly show, my seasonal acting gig also entailed keeping

110

the poor actor stuffed inside the blinding Paddington costume from bumping into walls and falling down the escalator as we journeyed through the halls of Macy's. Countless times a day, mothers would point to my furry sidekick in the galoshes and red felt coat and say, "Look, honey, Pooh Bear!" And I would correct them in my southern-infused cockney accent: "Oh, no. Pooh t'isn't ear. E az iz ed stuck in a tree. T'is Paddington Bear from Paddington Station, Ain-gland. At your service." My method acting won several fans and sold at least a dozen $9.95 bears during the holiday season.

Santacon

In 1994 the Cacophony Society staged the first SantaCon in San Francisco. This mass gathering of people clad in inexpensive Santa costumes celebrated the season in a distinctly anticommercial manner, mixing guerrilla street theater, pranksterism, and public intoxication. Recent SantaCon events have been held as far away as Antarctica. The event has also been called Santarchy, Santa Rampage, the Red Menace, and Santapalooza.

It also won me a spot in the parade.

Broadcast by NBC to some sixty million people, I knew it was my moment to be discovered. Surely I would stand out and hosts Willard Scott and Deborah Norville would spotlight me; I would end up with my own sitcom playing a British bobby. Unfortunately, neither happened.

It was the year blow-ups of Bart Simpson and Clifford the Big Red Dog joined the parade, and also the year Macy's introduced the "falloon." Rather than helium, the falloon was anchored to the float and pushed skyward by industrial strength cold-air fans. I was the British bobby–guinea pig beneath twenty-nine feet of inflatable nylon bear.

By the time I had made the two-and-a-half mile trek down Broadway to Herald Square, I'd smiled and waved to an estimated two million onlookers and had become a frozen chunk of "bobby" ice. But it mattered not. During my moment in the Jumbotron sun, there was a great poof of air from above and twenty-nine feet of Paddington Bear sat down atop me, suffocating my star-making moment. I spent the rest of my first Christmas in New York chaperoning Paddington Bear around Macy's.

The Windows

Like many people I met on my cross-country Christmas quest, who told me about their childhood Christmas-light-seeking expeditions, it was an annual tradition during my childhood as well. There was a fancy house on a pond owned by the local boiled peanut magnate that was always decked out for the holidays; we'd pile into the family van to see the sight with the carloads of other rubbernecking Christmas pilgrims. By the time we'd get our chance to circle the pond, our windows would be so steamed up it was like looking through backlit melted crayons.

Today a Christmas drive to look at the lights and decorations is still one of my annual traditions, only now it's in New York with a bunch of friends in the back of a stretch limo. Hosted by my first friend in the City, a fellow southerner named Jeff Stillwell, each year's limo ride is a defining moment of my holiday season.

Just a few years back, Jeff was the banquet manager of Windows on the World, the glamorous restaurant atop the World Trade Center. A couple of months before 9/11, he started a new job in a different location. Jeff lost thirty-four close friends that day. Each Christmas since,

the loss is a reminder for us to cherish each moment as we drive down Fifth Avenue singing carols and drinking champagne with our heads sticking out of the limo's sun roof.

During our Christmas ride, we stop along the way to peek at the magical, sometimes surreal, store windows, marveling at the creative inventiveness of their window dressers. Often smeared with the small handprints of children, these glass showcases are holiday fantasies—animated, detailed creations that leap to life like the illustrated pages of a great children's book.

Each year's themes are closely guarded secrets, and there is intense creative rivalry among those who create them. Lord & Taylor's flagship store on Fifth Avenue has taken precautions to the most extreme. Hydraulic lifts were installed so that the glitzy tableaux can be created below ground and lifted to street level at the designated unveiling time.

Like fashions on a runway, the lavish scenes created each year often set trends for future Christmas fancy in yards around the country.

Numerous famous artists have been discovered while creating behind the glass. Robert Rauschenberg and Jasper Johns, who became friends in New York City in the early 1950s, paid their rent by designing department store windows together under the name "Matson-Jones." Their talents were noticed and the rest is art history. The whimsical contributions of their contemporaries, most notably Linda Fargo of Bergdorf Goodman and Simon Doonan of Barneys, have made them synonymous with Christmas in New York and have made their windows the crown jewels of New York's Christmas.

The department stores in New York spare no expense, often spending millions of dollars to dress in their holiday best because, like the Christmassy houses and yards around the country, their store windows are gifts to passersby. And the whole world seems to pass by. The windows are so popular and such crowd pleasers that several stores have to hire personnel to direct the viewing lines.

Above the intersection of Fifty-seventh Street and Fifth Avenue hangs the world's largest outdoor crystal chandelier. Lighting designer Ingo Maurer created the snowflake for UNICEF. Six thousand tiny bulbs illuminate the more than two-and-a-half miles of twisted stainless steel used to create the snowflake;

twelve thousand Baccarat crystals create its dazzle. The snowflake was created to be a beacon of hope, peace, and compassion.

On the southeast corner of the block sits Saks Fifth Avenue. Spread across the facade of the ten-story building are huge LED-lit snowflakes, some twenty feet high. Each evening at 4:55 PM there is a shimmering fifteen-minute light show choreographed to "Carol of the Bells."

And on the northwest corner sits the sheer opulence and ravishing beauty of Bergdorf Goodman's windows with figures by sculptor Alexandra Limpert. The window stenciled "Entertain," in which a gowned woman opened the door to a black-tie-clad polar bear, was a stand-out favorite. It was a mesmerizing, fanciful fantasy that stopped pedestrians for much longer than the holiday rush should allow.

We end our limo tour each year walking through the Christmas wonderland that is Rockefeller Center.

The Tree

New York is the world's destination for Christmas, and Rockefeller Center, with its world famous tree and ice rink, is perhaps the planet's most photographed, videotaped, and filmed Christmas scene in the world. It has become a towering icon of Christmas.

Five Steps to a Gorgeous Tree

Creating the perfect Christmas tree is an art that can be broken down into five easy steps:

✳ DECORATE AWAY FROM THE WALL
You need to be able to access all sides. Pull out the tree and stand on a stepstool or ladder to reach the top branches.

✳ HANG THE LIGHTS FIRST
Start at the top and work your way down, keeping the lights plugged in if possible. Rather than simply circling the tree with lights, go in to the trunk and out along the branches as you work your way around. This will give the tree depth.

✳ HANG THE GARLAND
Again, start at the top and work your way around and down the tree, weaving the garland in and out and giving it swag.

✳ HANG THE ORNAMENTS, FROM BIG TO SMALL
If you have a lot of any one type of ornament, decorate with these first and space them evenly. If you have large ornaments, put them on early in the process to prevent the tree from looking unbalanced. Fill in with smaller ornaments, making sure not to ignore the inner branches of the tree as well as the tips.

✳ TOP IT OFF
The final touch is crowning the tree—otherwise it will look unfinished. Choose something that makes you happy, whether it be a big bow, a star, or an angel.

From the moment the tree is lit until Christmas, Rockefeller Center becomes a mecca for holiday seekers making a trek to the lights.

Millions of New Yorkers and visitors from around the globe walk the pathway lined with artist Valerie Clarebout's twelve wire-sculpted angels that lead from Fifth Avenue to the ice rink beneath the immense Rockefeller Center tree. The tree lighting is a nationally televised event.

The famous tree is carefully selected, often years in advance. Tree scouts searching for the perfect specimen take to the skies in helicopters; they fly throughout the northeast, as well as north to Canada and west to Ohio. The chosen tree is brought to New York on a custom-designed telescoping trailer and put in place by a crane; it is then adorned with thirty-thousand lights on five miles of wiring. The star at the top—9½ feet across and weighing 550 pounds—is the only ornament.

As I watch the ice skaters spin on the rink below and the tree twinkle above, visions of possibilities dance in my head. I am energized and inspired to make my own Christmas special—to assemble my Christmas treasures and decorate my Christmas trees in a unique way, however much smaller they are than Rockefeller Center's. My friends and I merrily go our separate ways to our homes and apartments to create our own winter wonderlands—wherever that is, and whatever that may mean for each of us.

Home for the Holidays

I grew up in the south, where decorating for Christmas is as expected as biscuits and gravy on Sunday morning. I've always taken to the holidays with verve and strive for perfection in my Christmas displays—as perfect as possible within the time and space available.

I've gotten my decorating routine down pretty well. I now spend the holiday at Edgewater Farm, my country escape in the Catskills, and Christmas there is, shall we say, *reflective*. I plant a forest of silver trees in my living room as a salute to the Christmases of my past.

Aluminum Trees

Evergleam, the original silver trees, were introduced by the Aluminum Specialty Company in Wisconsin in 1959. The trees were created as a way to use up all the extra postwar aluminum the company had. Due to the possibility of electric shock, lighting was provided by a rotating color wheel—a spotlight with three or four colored lenses that changed the color of the tree as the lens spun. Millions of the trees were purchased in the ten years they were manufactured, appealing to Space Age consumers; they have recently regained popularity.

My grandfather PaPa's house always had an aluminum Christmas tree—the one Lucy wanted Charlie Brown to find when he instead scored the scrub. It was always my Aunt Phyllis's job to decorate, and she made the most with what she had, creating a comforting, shimmering childhood vision—one that I try to re-create, however obsessively, with my significant stockpile of vintage ornaments.

I also always adorn a tree in my guest bedroom with the collection of ornaments that has been given to me each Christmas by my mother. Each year throughout childhood when it came time to decorate our tree, she'd present each of us with an ornament—Teddy bears for my brother, angels for my sister, and trains for me. Her heart still cries a little at the Christmas I laughed at her attempt to switch me from trains to Santas. "It's plastic," I said, in the brutal honesty of a thirteen-year-old. "I'd rather stick with trains."

Decades later she still talks about my snickering disdain at the plastic Santa. Though I now prize it as the uniquity in my collection, she stuck with trains, and each Christmas, whether I'm "at home" or "in New York," I receive a nicely wrapped train for my tree, dated in my mom's perfect schoolteacher handwriting. Like each Christmas memory, it is something forever cherished.

At my annual Night Before the Night Before Christmas Party, I recounted tales of the decorated

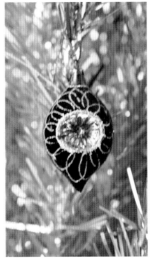

houses I'd seen all over the country and the people I met who spend thousands of dollars so that they can climb atop the house, risk life and limb, and create a gift for their neighbors. "So, why is it that people go to all that trouble?" one friend asked. I thought for a second. As I discovered, people decorate for a range of reasons, from honoring the memory of a lost daughter to the challenge of pushing a computer to its limits. So what did every single person have in common?

"They are kind people," I answered, "who believe in the magic of Christmas."

Decoration Destinations

ALABAMA

Christmas on the River: Since 1972, this nighttime Christmas parade floats down the nearby river in Demopolis. In addition to the river-worthy floats there is a fireworks show. Web site: www.demopolischamber.com/COTR/

Christmas Parade: For this popular Christmas parade in Bessemer participants decorate their cars and parade down the streets of the town. Web site: www.superpages.com/cities/mtg/10219/

ALASKA

Colony Christmas Celebration: This three-day festival in Alaska features a parade, reindeer-drawn sleigh rides, a Christmas triathlon, shopping, and more. Web site: www.palmerchamber.org/visiting/annual_events.asp

Talkeetna Winterfest: Many fun and unique activities take place during this month-long Christmas celebration, including the Bachelor Auction and Ball and the Wilderness Woman Contest (climbing a tree to escape a moose is just one of the events). Web site: www.talkeetnachamber.org/events.html

ARIZONA

Glendale Glitters Spectacular: This is Arizona's largest holiday light display, with an animated light show in addition to a "Winter Wonderland" with several tons of snow. Web site: www.glendaleaz.com/events/glendaleglittersspectacular.cfm

Red Rock Fantasy: Forty-five families in Sedona decorate their homes for this gorgeous display of popular cartoon characters. There's also a twenty-five-foot swan, among other features. Web site: www.redrockfantasy.com/index.html

World's Largest Gingerbread Village: For fourteen years this gingerbread village at the Prescott Resort has been the largest in the world. Web site: www.prescottresort.com/design.asp

ARKANSAS

Christmas Parade and Lights: Thousands of spectators come every year to the largest Christmas parade in the state. Throughout the season, El Dorado's downtown twinkles with lights and rings with caroling. Horse-drawn carriage rides are offered as well. Web site: www.boomtown.org/festivals.aspx

Trail of Holiday Lights: An annual tradition, the Trail of Holiday lights encompasses sixty-five communities in the state. In addition to the lights, features include food, music, parades, and other entertainment. Web site: www.arkansas.com/things-to-do/ trail-of-lights/

CALIFORNIA

Carols in the Caves: Christmas carols are played in caves throughout California each holiday season by the Improvisator, a musician who performs on up to two dozen instruments per performance. Audience members are invited to sing along. Web site: www.cavemusic.net

Christmas Tree Lane: A mile-long boulevard of 134 deodar cedar trees in Altadena was planted in 1885 and has been lighted annually at the holidays since 1920. It is recognized as the oldest large-scale outdoor Christmas display in the world and is listed in the National Register of Historic Places. Web site: www.christmastreelane.net

"The Glory of Christmas" at the Crystal Cathedral: An astounding one-of-a-kind Christmas pageant, complete with special effects, live animals, Christmas carols, and more. Web site: www.crystalcathedral.org/glory_christmas/ index.cfm

COLORADO

Denver Christkindl Market: A traditional German Christmas market, filled with unique Bavarian and European gifts. The season begins with a children's lantern parade and features fireworks and live music throughout the holidays. Web site: www.denverchristkindlmarket.com

The Molly Brown House Museum, Candlelight Tour & Reading: Enjoy a candlelight tour of the Molly Brown house while learning about Christmas traditions in Denver. The tour is followed by a reading of "A Visit From Saint Nicholas." Web site: http://mollybrown.org/specialevents2.esp

Parade of Lights: A major event in Denver, this spectacular display of lights is one of the most beautiful in the state. Web site: www.denverparadeoflights.com

CONNECTICUT

A Celebration of Lights and Song By the Sea: A Christmas tradition in New London, this festival includes music, a holiday market, and decorations, as well as other unique events including Santa and his reindeer arriving on a tugboat. Web site: http://newlondonmainstreet.org/events/lightsandsong2006.php

The Mark Twain House: Visitors can enjoy a special tour of the author's historic house in Hartford, which is decorated for the holidays every year in a Victorian style. Web site: www.marktwainhouse.org/calendar/index.php?id=607

DELAWARE

A Brandywine Christmas: A Victorian-style Christmas display, including an elaborate Victorian dollhouse, "critter" decorated Christmas trees, and an extensive O-gauge model railroad. Web site: www.visitdelaware.com/event .htm

Christmas Benefit Festival: This simple but lovely Christmas festival includes shopping, food, entertainment, and other activities. Web site: www.visitdelaware .com/event.htm

FLORIDA

Edison and Ford Winter Estates Holiday Houses: For more than thirty years these estates and gardens decorate their twenty acres with lights and displays that attract more than thirty thousand people annually. Web site: www.efwefla .org/hh.asp

Fort Lauderdale Christmas Pageant: A twenty-year tradition, this pageant offers a spectacular revue with carols, theater, and a re-enactment of the nativity and life of Christ. Web site: www.christmaspageant.info

Toys in the Sun Run: An annual event during which more than thirty thousand motorcyclists drive to a destination with the goal of collecting toys to donate to a children's hospital. Web site: www.toysinthesunrun.com

GEORGIA

Old-Fashioned Christmas: A town-wide event in Dahlonega, with a Christmas parade, Festival of Trees and Wreaths, tours, and more. Web site: web.georgia .org/net/calendar/details.aspx

Victorian Christmas, Downtown Thomasville: During the Christmas season this historic town gets decked out in Victorian finery. With carriage rides, a live nativity scene, music, and shopping, this award-winning event attracts many visitors every year. Web site: www.downtownthomasville.com

HAWAII

Gingerbread Festival: At this annual event held at the beginning of December, participants spend the day building gingerbread houses. Web site: www.blaisdell center.com

Honolulu City Lights: At this annual lighting of the Honolulu City Christmas tree, visitors enjoy decorations, live holiday music, and shopping, and watch the Public Workers' Electric Light Parade. Web site: www.honolulu.gov/csd/citylights/index.htm

IDAHO

Coeur d'Alene Resort Holiday Light Show: Aboard a ship on Lake Coeur d'Alene, visitors can view America's largest floating light show, a spectacular holiday parade, and a fireworks display—all in one night. Web site: www .visitidaho.org/thingstodo/events.aspx

Idaho Botanical Garden, Winter Garden aGlow: Every year the Idaho Botanical Garden celebrates the holiday season with a dazzling display of more than 250,000 lights. Web site: www.idahobotanicalgarden.org/index.cfm

ILLINOIS

Annual Christmas Tree Lighting Ceremony: This annual tree lighting of an eighty-five-foot-tall tree is the official kick off of the holiday season in Chicago. Daytime activities include shopping at a German Christkindlmarket, a visit to Santa's House, as well as other festivities. Web site: www.chicago traveler.com/chicago_festivals.htm

Hancock Holiday Mountain Railroad: While at the Hancock Observatory, check out this miniature display featuring twelve trains traveling more than fourteen hundred square feet of detailed and beautiful landscape that is decorated for the holidays. Web site: www.hancock-observatory.com/event.asp

The Magnificent Mile Lights Festival: Entertainment and fun abound at this annual event, the highlight of which is the lighting of one million lights along North Michigan Avenue in Chicago. Web site: www.themagnificentmile.com/SeasonalEvents/

INDIANA

Christmas in the Park: This event has been an honored tradition in Clay County since 1993. With a lighted Christmas Parade, a large light display, fireworks, breakfast with Santa, and more, it's easy to get into the holiday spirit. Web site: www.christmasinthepark.org

Santa Claus, Indiana: Every year the town of Santa Claus makes the most of its name, with numerous festivals and events in honor of Christmas, such as Santa's Candy Castle (the United States' first themed attraction), the Christmas Festival of Lights, the Nightmare Before Christmas golf tournament, a live nativity scene, and much more. Web site: www.legendaryplaces.org/events/christmasexperience.cfm

IOWA

Blossoms of Light Festival, Reiman Gardens: This exhibition of lights at Iowa State University features unique displays with a Scandinavian theme. Along with the lights, this festival also includes evening concerts, gardening demonstrations, and a visit from Santa Claus. Web site: www.reimangardens.com/index.cfm

Prelude to Christmas: Turn back time on Amana's candle-lit streets, and enjoy a seventeen-foot-tall German Christmas pyramid, live animated storybook characters, a craft bazaar, and a nativity scene. Web site: www.festivalsinamana.com

KANSAS

Santas Around the World: Every year twenty-two life-size, handcrafted Santas are prominently displayed at Santa World in Great Bend. Every piece features a different cultural depiction of Santa Claus in elaborate and traditional costumes, surrounded by a dazzling display. Web site: www.visitgreatbend.com/santaworld.htm

Trail of Lights: This event, also located in Great Bend, consists of three separate displays: Veteran's Park depicts the "Twelve Days of Christmas" in beautiful lights; Wild Lights, located at Brit Spaugh Park & Zoo, is an animal-themed exhibition; and the Lafayette Lights in Jack Kilby Square, which can be enjoyed while shopping or walking around. Web site: www.visitgreatbend.com/trailoflights.htm

Winter Wonderland: This must-see display features more than one million lights along two miles of road near Lake Shawnee. Web site: www.tarcinc.org/winter_promo.htm

KENTUCKY

Annual Old Fashion Country Christmas Show: The Kentucky Opry, a popular venue for country singers, hosts an annual country Christmas concert featuring everyone's favorite holiday songs. Notable performers include Garth Brooks, Trisha Yearwood, George Strait, Alan Jackson, and Alison Krause. Web site: www.kentuckyopry.com/special-events.asp

Light Up Louisville: This holiday celebration is more than just a lighting ceremony. For the entire day visitors can shop, watch a Winter Wonderland parade, and view Holiday Trees from Around the World, commemorating the holiday traditions of immigrants. The lighting itself is accompanied by fireworks and other entertainment. Web site: www.louisvilleky.gov/CommunityRelations/

Southern Lights, Spectacular Sights on Holiday Nights: This three-mile stretch of lights is just the beginning of the Southern Lights Christmas attraction. After viewing this spectacular display, visitors can ride the Mini-Train Express, go to the petting zoo and nearby museums, and much more. Web site: www.kyhorsepark.com/khp/holiday.

LOUISIANA

Christmas Festival of Lights: Christmas is no small thing in the historic town of Natchitoches. Parades, fireworks, light displays, shopping, food, and much more abound during this large and joyous celebration of the holiday season. Web site: www.christmasfestival.com

Christmas New Orleans Style: This festival is a real New Orleans–style celebration with bonfires, live holiday music, light displays, cooking demonstrations, good food, and more. Children can construct gingerbread houses and visit Santa while parents shop. There are also candlelight tours of decorated historic homes. Web site: http://fqfi.org/

MAINE

Christmas Prelude: The spirit of Maine is pervasive at this holiday celebration in Kennebunkport. Three tree-lighting ceremonies, a visit from Santa, a live nativity, and a bonfire, as well as shopping, food, entertainment, and more can all be found at this exciting festival. But while there, don't forget to watch the Cape Porpoise Lobster Tree Trap Lighting. Web site: www.christmasprelude.com

Sparkle Holiday Celebration: This event marks the beginning of the Christmas season in Freeport. This weekend-long festival is chockfull of fun activities—the annual parade, horse-drawn carriage rides, shopping, and a tuba-only Christmas concert. Web site: www.freeportusa.com/sparkle05.html

MARYLAND

Garden of Lights, Brookside Gardens: With more than six hundred thousand lights, the Brookside Gardens is a sight to behold during the holiday season. This walk-through display is one that families enjoy together year after year. Web site: www.mc-mncppc.org/parks/brookside/light.shtm

Winterfest of Lights: This festival, located in Ocean City, has a spectacular display of more than one million lights stretching over two miles. At the nearby Winterfest Village, visitors can drink hot cocoa, eat, and shop for souvenirs and Christmas presents. Web site: www.ococean.com/SEP.html

MASSACHUSETTS

Bright Nights at Forest Park: This immense lighting display is New England's most popular destination and features different "worlds" for viewers to discover, such as Jurassic World, Victorian Village, and Seuss Land. Web site: www.brightnights.org

Quincy Christmas Festival: This annual Christmas festival features a tree-lighting ceremony, a Christmas parade, a live nativity scene, and the arrival of Santa via parachute. Web site: http://ci.quincy.ma.us/xmasfestival.asp

Stockbridge Main Street at Christmas: Quaint Stockbridge's Main Street was made famous in a Norman Rockwell painting, and each year the town celebrates the artist by re-creating his popular work. Find music, food, theater, and more. Web site: www.stockbridgechamber.org/frxmas.html

MICHIGAN

Dickens Festival: Celebrate Christmas as Charles Dickens would have without traveling back in time. There are activities for both adults and children including game-show-style competitions, giant bubble making, and music. Web site: www.dickensfestivalholly.org

Dutch Winterfest and The Holidays in Downtown Holland: This two-week Europecentric holiday celebration kicks off with a parade of lanterns. Visitors can also enjoy a European Christmas market, food, music, and an ice-sculpting competition. Watch for Santa's helpers going around town giving out gifts or lumps of coal. Web site: www.holland.org

Wayne County Lightfest: With nearly a million lights covering four and a half miles, this display is understandably labeled "the Midwest's largest holiday light show." With animated displays and breathtaking designs, this event is a must-see. Web site: www.waynecounty.com/parks/seasonal.htm

MINNESOTA

Bentleyville Tour of Lights: This light display and festival began at the Esko home of Nathan Bentley. Along with spectacular lights, it now features a twenty-four-foot-tall castle of lights, a S'mores Hut, more than five hundred snowflakes, and visits from Santa. Web site: www.bentleyvilleusa.com

TCF Holidazzle Parade: A tradition since 1992, it is now an integral part of the holiday season in Minneapolis. Each year the parade adds new floats and characters to its lineup, from the Wizard of Oz to Captain Hook. Along with the main attraction, visitors can listen to community choirs outfitted in dazzling robes laced with hundreds of lights. Web site: www.holidazzle.com

MISSISSIPPI

Canton, City of Lights: Each year the city goes all out for Christmas. In addition to the Victorian Christmas festival, the Historic Courthouse Square is decorated with two hundred thousand lights. Other attractions include carousel rides, unique window displays, museums, a parade, and much more. Web site: www.cantontourism.com/victorian_xmas.html

Laurel Sertoma's Christmas Parade: The largest Christmas parade in Mississippi, this event happens every year on the first Saturday in December. It is not to be missed! In addition, Mason Park is decorated with more than eight hundred thousand lights and features live music and a visit from Santa. Web site: www.laurelms.com/attractions.html

Mistletoe Marketplace: This three-day fundraiser, held by the Junior League of Jackson, is the place to go for holiday shopping, entertainment, and cooking demonstrations. Web site: www.jljackson.org/

MISSOURI
Holiday Magic, Lake of the Ozarks: This lake resort area features a drive-through park with two miles of lighted and animated displays as well as light tunnels. Web site: www.lakeholidaymagic.com

Kansas City's Holiday Festival: This annual festival is packed with activities for the whole family. Food, shopping, ice carving, horse-drawn sleigh rides, and lots of decorations can be found at this fun-filled event. Web site: www .downtownkc.org/

MONTANA
Billings Holiday Parade and Christmas Stroll: Enjoy holiday festivities in downtown Billings during the annual Christmas parade. Then take the Billings Christmas Stroll—a fifty-year tradition—to view decorations in the downtown area. Web site: www.downtownbillings.com/christmas

Christmas Eve Torchlight Parade with Santa: Every year in Whitefish, Santa Claus and his helpers arrive in style with an amazing torchlight parade through the village. Santa gives out toys to children. Web site: www.whitefishchamber .com/whitefish_events.php

NEBRASKA
Journey into Christmas, The Bess Streeter Aldrich House: The historic house of one of Nebraska's most celebrated authors is decked out for the holidays. Visitors can take a self-guided tour. Web site: www.lincolnne.com/nonprofit/bsaf/

Old-Fashioned Downtown Christmas: This local holiday celebration is one that families can enjoy every year with food, entertainment, storytelling, pony rides, and more make. Web site: www.downtowngi.com/events.htm

NEVADA

Country Christmas Faire: Held at the Nevada County Fairgrounds, this festival offers a wide selection of gourmet food, crafts, shopping, live music, and holiday contests such as gingerbread-house design and Christmas cooking. Web site: www.nevadacountyfair.com/HTMLS/aachmas.html

Hidden Valley Parade of Lights: Many visitors come to enjoy the spectacular displays of twinkling lights, nativity scenes, and snowmen created by the residents of this neighborhood. Be on the lookout for wild horses that roam the streets. Web site: http://renotahoe.about.com/b/a/133327.htm

NEW HAMPSHIRE

Polar Express: Children and adults alike can take a ride on the Polar Express from New Hampshire to the North Pole. This evening event re-creates the story of the popular children's book—the adventures of one little boy on his way to the North Pole. Web site: www.polarexpress.org

Santa's Village: This Christmas-themed park has everything any visitor, young or old, could imagine. There are Christmas-themed rides such as Santa's Skyway Sleigh and Santa's Antique Cars as well as a 3-D movie "Tinkerdoodle Christmas," and lots of lights. Web site: www.santasvillage.com/christmas.html

NEW JERSEY

Dickens Festival: Inspired by Charles Dickens's work *A Christmas Carol,* this festival is the kickoff of the holiday season for the town of Medford. Events include the arrival of Santa Claus, the tree-lighting ceremony, and a live nativity scene. Web site: www.hmva.org/festivals.html

The Elvis House: This display of Christmas lights and famous characters in Mahwah has become a New Jersey holiday legend. It all started when William Maloney put a life-size statue of Elvis on his roof. Next, Marilyn Monroe climbed up, followed by Charlie Chaplin and Laurel and Hardy. The neighborhood has joined in to make this a must-see Christmas spectacle. Web site: www.williammaloney.com/Misc/Christmas/2004/

NEW MEXICO

Albuquerque River of Lights: Every year the Rio Grande Botanic Garden presents an outstanding light display at this largest light show in the state. This walk-through experience features ingenious light sculptures and hundreds of thousands of lights. Web site: www.cabq.gov/biopark/garden/educationlights.html

Farolito Walk in Santa Fe: For a few hours each Christmas Eve cars are forbidden and all electric lights are turned off in the downtown area, so that the candlelight of the farolitos, or lanterns, can be enjoyed in all their splendor. They are placed by the thousands on rooftops and sidewalks, transforming the adobes into luminous silhouettes. Web site: www.santafe.com/travel/christmas.html

NEW YORK

Bronx Zoo Holiday Lights: The zoo sparkles with more than 140 illuminated animal sculptures plus snowflakes, starbursts, more than eight miles of lighted trees, and more than two miles of lighted buildings. Web site: www.bronxzoo.com

Rockefeller Center Christmas Tree: The world's most famous Christmas tree—usually between sixty-five and ninety feet tall—is a spectacular mountain of branches covered with thirty thousand lights on five miles of wire. Web site: www.rockefellercenter.com

NORTH CAROLINA

Christmas at Biltmore: In Asheville, Christmas at America's largest home is one of the premier holiday events of the season. Enjoy the breathtaking decorations and candlelight celebrations. Web site: www.biltmore.com/plan/calendar/calendar_holiday.shtml

Christmas Town USA: McAdenville gets decked out for Christmas with more than 375 decorated Christmas trees. Recognized by many talk and news shows, the town has been decorating since 1956. Web site: www.mcadenville christmastown.com

Home for the Holidays: The small town of Hendersonville celebrates Christmas with a wonderful festival, including theater, music, a historic homes tour, and decorations to delight every member of the family. Web site: www.historic henderson-ville.org/holidays.htm

NORTH DAKOTA

Lights on Broadway Parade: Everyone in the family will enjoy this holiday light parade of flashy floats going down Broadway Avenue in Bismarck. Web site: www.downtownbismarck.com

Medora's Cowboy Christmas: Dancing, food, parades, and Christmas lights—these are just a few things visitors can partake in and see. Medora's Cowboy Christmas features horse-drawn wagon rides, old-fashioned decorations, and even a stick-horse rodeo. Web site: www.medorand.com/xmas.htm

OHIO

Christmas Candlelightings: Roscoe Village starts the Christmas season with this popular festival. During the day music, food, carriage rides, and other activities entertain visitors. At night the Christmas tree is lit during a special ceremony involving every member of the crowd. Web site: www.roscoevillage.com

Christmas on the Green: Join in with the Christmas celebrations in Piqua. This event features beautiful decorations, horse-drawn carriage rides, a visit from Santa, bonfires, and much more. Web site: www.ohiotraveler.com

"A Christmas Story" House: Enter the setting for the movie of the same name—one of the most famous Christmas films of all time. With tours, holiday events and activities, and more, the Christmas spirit is abundant at this popular tourist destination. Web site: www.achristmasstoryhouse.com

OKLAHOMA

Downtown in December: This annual event in downtown Oklahoma City is host to many winter and holiday activities for visitors of all ages. Light displays, snow-tubing rides down the nation's largest man-made slope, a botanical garden display, and much more are featured during this exciting month-long event. Web site: www.downtownokc.com

Pryor Parade of Lights: Every year this massive parade features floats with more than one hundred different holiday scenes and displays. Web site: www.pryorok.com

OREGON

Christmas Festival of Lights: This popular holiday event is held at a Catholic shrine and botanical garden located in Portland. With an angel-covered cliffside as a backdrop, ecumenical lighting, and six thousand singers this event brings the true spirit of Christmas to every visitor. Web site: www.thegrotto.org/events/lights.htm

Magical Murals: Eighteen gigantic fiber-optic musical Christmas murals light up the city of Grants Pass each holiday season. Each mural tells a holiday story in thirty seconds. Web site: www.grantspassoregon.gov/index.aspx?page=315

PENNSYLVANIA

Christkindlmarkt Bethlehem: This Christmas market, held in the city of Bethlehem, is full of wonders for visitors to look at, eat, and buy during the holiday season. It features the crafts of more than one hundred artisans as well as live holiday music. Web site: www.christkindlmarkt.org

Koziar's Christmas Village: Nicknamed "the greatest Christmas display in the USA," the amazing displays and spectacular lights are sure to wow every visitor. This Christmas event is a must-see. Web site: www.koziarschristmas village.com

RHODE ISLAND

Christmas in Newport: For more than thirty years Newport has reveled in the spirit of Christmas with this outstanding festival. It includes horse tours, a Christmas train, food, entertainment, shopping, and more. The city's wharves and harbor are lighted—an especially lovely nighttime sight. Web site: www.christmasinnewport.org

Festival of Lights: Enjoy the thousands of lights adorning the small town of Wickford Village during the holiday season. Visitors can also enjoy hayrides, window-decorating competitions, live holiday music, and other entertainment. Web site: www.wickfordvillage.org

SOUTH CAROLINA

The Carolina Opry Christmas Special: This annual Christmas spectacular attracts thousands of visitors. With dancing, singing, comedy, and holiday merriment, this production truly embodies the festive Christmas spirit of South Carolina. Web site: www.cgp.net/ChristmasSpecial.html

Christmas in Charleston: Christmas is big in this city. Each year it hosts numerous holiday events, including Christmas markets, holiday tours, a reindeer run, parades, and much more. Web site: www.christmasincharleston.com

SOUTH DAKOTA

Christmas at the Capitol: This festival kicks off the state's holiday season. Spectacular Christmas displays, ninety decorated trees, a pie competition, and

other fun activities makes this a much-anticipated annual event. Web site: www.state.sd.us/governor/trees2006/default.aspx

Jingle in the Jungle: This unusual but exciting event takes place each year at Reptile Gardens, which has the largest reptile collection in the world. Filled with Christmas flowers, this display is truly unusual and delightful. Web site: www.reptilegardens.com/jingleinthejungl.html

TENNESSEE
The Enchanted Garden of Lights: This amazing light display, located just outside of Chattanooga, highlights massive ancient rock formations. With nightly live music and entertainment, this walk-through event features more than a half-million holiday lights and twenty-five holiday scenes. Web site: www .seerockcity.com/Flash/garden.htm

Tennessee Plantation Christmas Tour: Visitors learn about Christmas on a plantation while taking a horse-drawn wagon ride. They also view decorations, learn traditional carols, and enjoy refreshments. Web site: www.cityofgood lettsville.org

TEXAS
Christmas in the Stockyards: The Fort Worth Stockyards celebrate the holiday season with an annual event that features the lighting of a forty-foot-tall pine tree, an annual horseback "Ride for Toys," and of course, the Cattle Drive followed by a holiday parade. Web site: www.christmasinthestockyards.com

Trail of Lights, Austin: First celebrated in 1965, this annual festival marks the beginning of the holiday season with the lighting of a sensational mile-long light display. This event features the "World's Largest Man Made Tree," an attraction definitely worth seeing. Web site: www.ci.austin.tx.us/tol

Wonderland of Lights, Marshall, Texas: In the spirit of peace and brotherhood, Marshall presents a holiday extravaganza with nearly ten million lights! The historic Harrison County Courthouse, located in the center of the Downtown Square, is the festival's "crown jewel" with more than 125,000 tiny white lights. Web site: www.holidaytrailoflights.com/marshall.html

UTAH

Christmas Utah: This cheerful, fun-filled light display features over one hundred thousand lights synchronized to music—perfect for young and old alike. Web site: www.christmasutah.com

Jubilee of Trees: There are more than trees to rejoice about at the Jubilee of Trees. This festival has all sorts of fun activities: a fashion show, a teddy bear picnic, a tree auction, and much more. Web site: www.jubileeoftrees.org

VERMONT

The Santa Express: This holiday train ride from White River Junction to Thetford is fun for the whole family. Children are treated to a gift from Santa and Mrs. Claus. Web site: www.rails-vt.com/gmf_santa.html

Stowe Festival of Trees: Displays of decorated Christmas trees, each representing a different culture or country from around the world, are featured at this lovely event. Web site: www.vtliving.com/events/dec.shtml

VIRGINIA

Christmas in Williamsburg: Colonial Williamsburg decks itself out for this holiday celebration with miles of pine roping, bushels of fruit, and truckloads of greenery. Learn about Colonial Christmas traditions and enjoy entertainment and activities, such as wreath making and the "Grand Illumination" with fireworks and a spectacle of candles. Web site: www.history.org/christmas

Tacky Light Tour: The houses on this tour in Richmond feature lights galore—the more, the merrier. Each house on the mapped-out tour must have at least thirty thousand tacky Christmas lights to qualify. A must-see! Web site: www.tackylighttour.com

WASHINGTON

Christmas in Leavenworth: In the small town of Leavenworth, Christmas is one of the busiest times of the year. Many of the residents have a Bavarian background and all activities—from Christmas concerts, bazaars, a lantern parade, and more—reflect this heritage. Web site: www.leavenworth.org/events/december.html

Zoolights: This creative animal-themed light display can be found at the Point Defiance Zoo in Tacoma. Visitors walk through the display while enjoying refreshments and live holiday music. Web site: www.pdza.org

WEST VIRGINIA

Oglebay Winter Festival of Lights: This display, recognized as one of the biggest and best in the country, has drawn visitors since 1985. Visitors drive through six miles of beautiful lights. Web site: www.oglebay-resort.com/fol.htm

Yuletide in the Park: This Christmas celebration is one that families can enjoy every holiday season. Activities include bonfires, hayrides, arts and crafts, Christmas lights, and a "Reindog" parade featuring dogs sporting Christmas costumes and antlers. Web site: www.putnam county.org/parks/yuletide.htm

WISCONSIN

Country Christmas Light Show: Visitors can view more than 250 light displays in celebration of the Christmas season along a drive-through trail in Waukesha. Web site: www.travelwisconsin.com/Fairs_and_Festivals.aspx

Milwaukee Holiday Lights Festival: This beautiful light festival features sporting events, live holiday music, historic tours, and the biggest display of Christmas lights in the city. Web site: www.milwaukeeholidaylights.com

WYOMING

Cheyenne Christmas Parade: This annual parade—considered a highlight of the holiday season—features colorful floats, horse-drawn wagons, antique cars, and more. Web site: www .cheyennenetwork.com/christmasparade

Christmas Opening and Parade of Lights: The lighting of Pioneer Square in November marks the beginning of the holiday season here. Visitors can gorge themselves at the chili feed, enjoy the parade, and watch the fireworks at this family-friendly festival. Web site: www.wyomingtourism.org/discover_ wyoming/events/

"A Visit From Saint Nicholas"
by Clement Clarke Moore

This famous story was first published anonymously on December 23, 1823, in the *Troy (NY) Sentinel*. Later attributed to Clement Clarke Moore, it established Santa Claus as an American icon.

'Twas the night before Christmas, when all through the house

Not a creature was stirring, not even a mouse;

The stockings were hung by the chimney with care,

In hopes that St. Nicholas soon would be there;

The children were nestled all snug in their beds,

While visions of sugar-plums danced in their heads;

And mamma in her 'kerchief, and I in my cap,

Had just settled our brains for a long winter's nap,

When out on the lawn there arose such a clatter,

I sprang from the bed to see what was the matter.

Away to the window I flew like a flash,

Tore open the shutters and threw up the sash.

The moon on the breast of the new-fallen snow

Gave the lustre of mid-day to objects below,

When, what to my wondering eyes should appear,

But a miniature sleigh, and eight tiny reindeer,

With a little old driver, so lively and quick,

I knew in a moment it must be St. Nick.

More rapid than eagles his coursers they came,

And he whistled, and shouted, and called them by name;

"Now, Dasher! now, Dancer! now, Prancer and Vixen!

On, Comet! on, Cupid! on, Donder and Blitzen!

To the top of the porch! to the top of the wall!

Now dash away! dash away! dash away all!"

As dry leaves that before the wild hurricane fly,

When they meet with an obstacle, mount to the sky;

So up to the house-top the coursers they flew,

With the sleigh full of Toys, and St. Nicholas too.

And then, in a twinkling, I heard on the roof

The prancing and pawing of each little hoof.

As I drew in my head, and was turning around,

Down the chimney St. Nicholas came with a bound.

He was dressed all in fur, from his head to his foot,

And his clothes were all tarnished with ashes and soot;

A bundle of Toys he had flung on his back,

And he looked like a peddler just opening his pack.

His eyes—how they twinkled! his dimples how merry!

His cheeks were like roses, his nose like a cherry!

His droll little mouth was drawn up like a bow

And the beard of his chin was as white as the snow;

The stump of a pipe he held tight in his teeth,

And the smoke it encircled his head like a wreath;

He had a broad face and a little round belly,

That shook when he laughed, like a bowlful of jelly.

He was chubby and plump, a right jolly old elf,

And I laughed when I saw him, in spite of myself;

A wink of his eye and a twist of his head,

Soon gave me to know I had nothing to dread;

He spoke not a word, but went straight to his work,

And filled all the stockings; then turned with a jerk,

And laying his finger aside of his nose,

And giving a nod, up the chimney he rose;

He sprang to his sleigh, to his team gave a whistle,

And away they all flew like the down of a thistle,

But I heard him exclaim, ere he drove out of sight,

"Happy Christmas to all, and to all a good-night."

ACKNOWLEDGMENTS

To all those who decorate with gusto, thank you for keeping childhood wonder alive. To each of the families who shared their holidays with me, thank you for your spirit and your kindness, and to my own family, especially Mom and Pop, my heart is warmed by the memories of many Christmases with you.

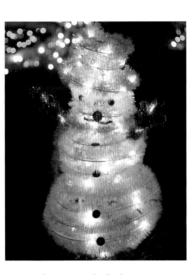

This book would be dark if not for the brilliant eye of photographer Cal Crary, who traveled the country with me and convinced me to go "triptic" and "diptic." We spent a Christmas together that I will always treasure.

My intern Britt Carpenter is an amazing talent. Trust me, her name will be in lights. Thanks to journalism teacher Jennifer Mitchell, who brought us together.

Much love to Mary and Tim Cleary, for all you are and all you do; to Deb Drucker, for giving me the best gift of all; to Ian Lane and Rochelle Riservato, for always coming through; and to Jeff Gautier, for making me look good. A big hug to Jeff Stillwell and Kim Bloodworth for starting the Christmas-in-New York limo tradition. And to the cast of characters I get to share the holidays with, I adore each of you.

To Dianne Chinnes, thanks for being the president of my fan club and for all you have done to inspire my success. And to Beth Phibbs, a big wink for telling me I should be a writer.

To Barbara Corcoran, for all the lessons you have taught me, the leg up you gave me, and your special friendship, which is ever-cherished.

I am appreciative to historian Tom Kelleher, curator of Old Sturbridge Village, for sharing his Christmas wisdom with me. And for

those who kindly provided photos: Victor Ovalle and the Austin Parks and Recreation Department, pages 74–76; Holly Shrewsbury and the Denver Botanic Garden, pages 72, 78–80; Darin McGregor, *Rocky Mountain News*, page 81; John Blom and the Newport Chamber of Commerce, page 82; and Michael Liquori, pages 106–107.

I'm honored to be represented by agent Todd Shuster at Zachary Shuster Harmsworth, a true gentleman, and attorney Eric Brown, the kindest pit bull in New York. Thanks always to publicity legend, Sy Presten, whose typewriter is well connected.

I am blessed to work with an amazing group of people at HarperCollins: publisher Marta Schooler, a visionary; art director Ilana Anger and designer Kay Schuckhart, brilliant artists; one-in-a-million publicist Gretchen Crary; Dinah Fried and Margarita Vaisman, the mover and the shaker; Felicia Sullivan, web genius; Angie Lee, marketing genius; George Bick and the incredible sales force; Tricia Levi, the sharpshooter; and lastly, my editor, Liz Sullivan, who was appropriately cast as Lucy in her school "Charlie Brown Christmas" play, "Good grief!" is she good.

My most special Christmas wishes to North Shore Animal League for giving me my two greatest gifts and excellent writing partners: Jasper and Westminster.

And to Scott Stewart, who helps make my adulthood as fun as my childhood, I am honored to be your best friend.

Peace on earth. And good will toward *everyone*.